An Administrator's Guide —

LEADING WITH INTEGRITY

Reflections on Legal, Moral and Ethical Issues in School Administration

Clarence G. Oliver, Jr., Ed.D.

authorHOUSE®

AuthorHouse™
1663 Liberty Drive
Bloomington, IN 47403
www.authorhouse.com
Phone: 1 (800) 839-8640

Published by AuthorHouse 11/30/2015

ISBN: 978-1-5049-6207-0 (sc)
ISBN: 978-1-5049-6208-7 (hc)
ISBN: 978-1-5049-6206-3 (e)

Library of Congress Control Number: 2015919110

Other Books By
Clarence G. Oliver, Jr.

Ethical Behavior
An Administrator's Guide:
Ethics and Values in School Administration

One from the Least
And Disappearing Generation:
A Memoir of a Depression-Era Kid

Tony Dufflebag . . .
and Other Remembrances
of the War in Korea

Broken Arrow: The First Hundred Years
(Contributing Author and Co-Editor)

The History of Broken Arrow
Documentary DVD Movie
(Storyline Author and Movie Narrator)

A Time of Peace, Season of Innocence . . .
Young People in a Small Town in Oklahoma
Between World War II and The Korean War

"Always do right.
This will gratify some people
and astonish
the rest."

—Mark Twain
(Samuel Longhorne Clemens)
1835-1910

Contributions By

Members of the Ethics Committee
Oklahoma Association of School Administrators

Rick Garrison, Chairman
   Superintendent of Schools
   Cheyenne Public Schools

Dr. Jim Beckham
   Superintendent of Schools
   Blanchard Public Schools

Cliff Johnson
   Superintendent of Schools
   Latta Public Schools

Contents

THE PUBLIC TRUST—

". . . all public officials and public employees are agents of the people and hold their positions for the benefit of the people. They are bound to uphold the Constitution of the United States and the Constitution of this state and to perform efficiently and faithfully their duties under the laws of the federal, state and local governments. Such officers and employees must observe, in their official acts, high standards of ethics regardless of personal consideration, recognizing that promoting the public interest and maintaining the respect for their government must be a foremost concern."

—Oklahoma Statutes

THE VISION—

Our nation needs school administrators who are ethical, honest, gracious, bold, strong, devoted educators who are filled with a love for children and have a desire to provide for them the very best in educational opportunities and services.

Purposes of the Book—

- To cultivate awareness that sound ethics is essential for survival in the 21st Century.
- To provide a language for talking about ethics and to encourage discussion of ethical issues.
- To provide practical experience in developing a set of values that reflects a group's common ethical ground.
- To promote ethical fitness by providing practical tools to use in dealing with difficult dilemmas.
- To develop an understanding of the difference between right and wrong and the rationale for making ethical decisions.
- To promote moral courage and identify how moral courage plays a part in decision-making.

DEDICATION—

In Appreciation of Steven Crawford—

Throughout his four decades long career as a teacher, administrator, superintendent, and executive director of the Oklahoma Association of School Administrators and the Cooperative Council of Oklahoma School Administration, Steven Crawford has been a strong proponent of ethical conduct and civility on the part of all who are entrusted as leaders at all levels of education. This book is a reflection of his belief that school administrators who lead and serve in communities across the land must demonstrate trustworthiness in all that they do and say. The author and the OASA Ethics Committee members who share reflections on "Legal, Moral and Ethical Issues" in this book hope to advance that belief and are pleased to dedicate this work to him and in his honor.

Prologue —

School administrators encounter situations—almost on a daily basis—that require personal judgments to be made that involve ethical decisions. For those decisions to be reached almost automatically, though, one must have internalized a solid legal, moral and ethical values system.

Often, one has an instinctive feeling or intuition—some call a "gut feeling"—of what is right or wrong, and speak or act accordingly. Without that personal compass to keep a person always moving in the right direction, it is easy to stumble. What follows can be as minor as a slight embarrassment or can reach the level of criminal prosecution and significant punishment.

Each of is created with an internal "monitor" that acts as a moral compass. Most call is our "conscience." Some people mistakenly think that the conscience is God's voice. In reality, it is God's gift to each of us. That special personal compass helps guide us on life's journey and points to standards of right and wrong that can help guide our decisions.

If that internal compass that tells us what is "right" has been programmed incorrectly, with wrong teachings, our conscious can nudge us in the wrong directions.

Ideally, the internalized ethical and values system was started during early childhood with instructions from parents, grandparents, other relatives, school teachers, school administrators, Sunday school teachers, church leaders, and other adult models who influenced us either by teaching or example or both. Those experiences helped each of us embrace a set of principles, making it possible for us to sense what is right and wrong.

Some might say that a person with a properly programmed internal compass has "scruples," experiencing a doubt or hesitation that troubles the conscience when there is some difficulty determining whether some pending decision or act is "right" or "wrong."

Having scruples is good!

If one has some hesitation, some reservation, some misgiving about a considered action, then most likely the considered decision or action is wrong—if your moral compass is properly programmed.

School administrators must be certain that his or her internal monitor, compass or conscience is finely tuned to the highest standards. Unfortunately, many leaders do not have a properly functioning moral compass.

Each of us can learn through observing both good and bad examples, recognizing how some leaders before us made some bad decisions as well as some good decisions. The consequences of those good and bad decisions are recorded in history—if not in books, perhaps in newspapers or stories passed down to others. The good behavior can be embraced. The bad behavior can be ignored.

Several years ago, one of Oklahoma's great political writers and strategists, the late Martin Hauan, wrote a very interesting book about how to "beat the system" in Oklahoma politics. The book was titled, *How to Win Elections Without Hardly Cheatin' At All.*[1]

Hauan, in talking about the book, once said, "Some of the politicians I've worked with are among the craftiest, most colorful and creative to ever set foot in the campaign ring."

He described them as "saints and sinners, even as you and I."

Hauan included school administrators in that "even as you and I" comment about "saints and sinners."

In his book, Hauan told stories about how some well-known and some not-so-well-known Oklahomans sort of skirted around the law in the climb to success in Oklahoma politics. There are some really interesting chapter titles in the book—such as "Lowest and best bidder," "Justice for Sale," "Tangled Web," "Things I Could Go to Hell for," "Don't Sweat the Small Stuff," "Senator Reachout," etc.

One day, while visiting with an executive of one of the state's most successful public relations firms, I discussed the project of this book dealing with school administrators facing so many "ethical and moral issues" and how they should demonstrate "integrity" in their behavior as they lead in a school district. During the conversation I shared the story of Hauan's unique book title; and, the PR executive with whom I was visiting suggested using part of that title, "without hardly cheatin' at all," as a focus of the study of ethics.

---

[1] Hauan, Martin. *How to Win Elections Without Hardly Cheatin' At All.* Oklahoma City, Oklahoma: Midwest Political Publications, 1983.

I thought about it, but then decided that the "tongue in cheek" title might leave a hint—even a very subtle impression—that "a little cheating" is okay. I didn't want to leave that impression; so, that idea was tossed out the window. Cheating simply is not an option.

Ethical behavior should be the foundation of everything a school administrator does. The administrator should act not only in compliance with the law, regulations and policies, but also always in an ethical manner. Administrators often have discretion in decision-making. In those situations, the decisions should be lawful, ethical, and morally right. Always "do the right thing." Sometimes, that means not only observing law or policy, but also reaching even beyond those minimum requirements by "walking the second mile."[2]

Ethics is serious business, and should be considered as such. It is through appropriate ethical behavior that trust is built. School leaders must not only observe the laws of the land but also must make decisions on the basis of ethical and moral values.

Because the public welfare is at issue, there are laws and regulations which have been written and which provide legal instructions for many decisions which administrators face. But, what about those times where there aren't clearly-stated statutes or other standards for behavior?

Most of us learned early in life that the Bible is a very good guidebook for living, in addition to containing its spiritual message. Here is an example concerning a good reason to act in accordance with solid legal and ethical standards—simply

---

[2] *The Holy Bible*, Matthew 5:41, New International Version, Grand Rapids: Zondervan House, 1984.

doing what is right. The writer, the Apostle Paul, in a letter to people living in Rome, wrote:

> *"For rulers hold no terror for those who do right, but for those who do wrong. Do you want to be free from fear of the one in authority? Then do what is right and he will commend you."*
> —*Romans 13:3. (NIV)*

The message is simple: Do what is right and you will not have to be fearful of accusations or punishment from those in authority, but may even be commended for your behavior.

Hopefully, information in this book will offer a bit of guidance, assistance and encouragement. The book sets forth a few standards that should guide the behavior of school administrators as they lead with integrity.

Serving as a school administrator is a public service and those who are chosen must be good stewards, worthy of the public trust. In all your endeavors, whether official or personal, always take the surest path—the high road.

Clarence G. Oliver, Jr.,
Ed.D.
2015

CHAPTER ONE

A Starting Thought — Integrity

Judge me, O Lord;
for I have walked in mine integrity:
I have trusted also in the Lord;
therefore I shall not slide.
—Psalms 26:1

There are several core tenets for Leadership. Among them are these—Integrity, Fairness, and Trust. Although there must be a commitment to all three of the core values, the one among these fundamental principles that rises to a primary position is Integrity. To that one tenet, the commitment must be absolute.

But, what is "Absolute" Integrity?

As an adjective, "absolute" adds emphasis, meaning that the noun, "integrity," is unequivocal or unconditionally embraced.

All those individuals who diligently serve with a leader—whether in staff positions, in subordinate leadership roles, in classrooms, or any other assignments—will forgive a leader for some mistakes. The one failure that is unforgivable in a leader's behavior, though, is a lack of integrity. Failure to lead with integrity is deplorable. It is virtually unpardonable.

Dr. William A. Cohen, in writing on the topic, declared, "Absolute integrity is the basis of heroic leadership."[3]

Another writer, a long-time school administrator and professor, Dr. Kerry Roberts, focused on "honesty" with his observation, "A superintendent of integrity is an honest person. They do not lie, steal, cheat, or treat employees unfairly. The true follower of Christ has little problem with these major issues. Even the best superintendent, however, can sometimes be careless about integrity in little things. It is important they maintain their integrity at every level."

With a reference to the writings of an ancient King of Israel, Dr. Roberts explained that those little careless acts are like "the little foxes that spoil the vines." (Song of Solomon 2:15).

Integrity has a finer point, though. Dr. Roberts observed that the root word for integrity is "integer," which implies singleness, unity, something, not divided, consistency, and by extension, reliability and trustworthiness — in everything.[4]

The superintendent of integrity presents the same face every time and in every situation. In contrast, a hypocrite presents a different face to different people. Even a little two-facedness violates principles and undermines integrity. Those who observe this behavior lose the ability to trust the leader.

---

[3] Cohen, William A. *Heroic Leadership*. John Wiley and Sons, Inc., Hoboken, New Jersey, 2010.

[4] Roberts, Kerry; Sampson, Pauline and Glenn, Jeremy, *Daily Devotionals for Superintendents*, Nacogdoches, Texas: Stephen F. Austin State University Press, 2014.

Without integrity, a leader cannot succeed. That is especially true for the individuals who serve as superintendents of schools, or in other school leadership roles.

> *"I walk a road less traveled, to a vision few men see. The road is straight and narrow but leads to integrity. The journey is quite easy when all eyes are focused on me. But it's what I do when I'm alone which defines integrity."*
> —*Author Unknown*

CHAPTER TWO

Moral Character —

> *"A good name is to be*
> *more desired than great wealth,*
> *favor is better than silver and gold."*
> *—Proverbs 22:1*

Leaders in many school districts have introduced into the curriculum some character-building programs in an effort to encourage students to embrace standards or principles of good behavior . . . or moral character. The students are encouraged to develop good habits that are modeled after examples of appropriate behavior. Exemplary individuals in society sometimes are pointed to as role models.

Unfortunately, the young people who are being encouraged to embrace high moral character traits sometimes look around and see adults who seem to have grown accustomed to shrugging off lapses in moral character as evidenced in the secretive and deceptive lifestyles reported in the media or observed in behavior of people in positions of leadership or authority.

Some cynics have implied that trying to find people who value honesty and model responsibility, who promote fairness, accountability, loyalty, respect for others, and who hold to strong, upright convictions is not at all realistic.

In the minds of some, the people who truly live such commendable life style "do not exist." In the midst of a national election a few years ago, when vicious negative advertising appeared daily in political television commercials, one political journalist wrote this sarcastic "blog" comment: "We are voting for a President, not a Pope!" [5]

Dr. Charles R. Swindoll, one of the nation's best-known religious leaders, reflected on the negativism of the "blog" and the attitude that high standards and behavior aren't unimportant. He said of the analogy, "Nonsense!" He added, "That kind of logic, or rather, lack of logic, gives me the jitters."[6]

This respected pastor, author, educator, radio and television preacher, seminary president and chancellor, as well as a U. S. Marine Corps veteran in Southeast Asia, knows whereof he speaks. During the half-century spent encouraging people through speaking and writing, Dr. Swindoll has encountered the "good" and the "bad" in society, and he rightly believes the preponderance of people in this great nation value honesty, responsibility, promote fairness, demonstrate loyalty, respect for others, and hold to strong, upright convictions.

The pillars of character that students are being taught in the classroom need to be embraced and modeled by every school administrator the young people see each day. Being

---

[5] Hack Wilson Blog. Tuesday, February 21, 2012. http://hackwilson.blogspot.com/2012/we-are-voting-for-president-not-pope.html

[6] Swindoll, Charles R. *Wisdom for the Way*, J. Countryman, a division of Thomas Nelson, Inc., Nashville, Tennessee, 2001.

trustworthy, respectful, responsible, fair, caring and good citizens are fine standards. But, these are just "the start" toward being solidly grounded ethically and morally.

Every school administrator needs to be the most visible exemplary model for students to observe of an adult whose daily walk demonstrates high moral standards and ethical behavior. Failure of administrators to be such role models should be viewed as dereliction of duty.

CHAPTER THREE

Goals Behind Study of Ethics

Discussion of ethics and ethical behavior by administrators—or members of any profession, for that matter—should be undertaken in an effort to cultivate an awareness that sound ethics is essential for survival in society. Such study should focus on several goals, provides a common language for talking about ethics and encourages discussion of ethical issues—especially within professional groups.

The study and discussion among professionals assist in developing a set of values that reflects a group's common ethical ground and promote a feeling of ethical fitness by providing practical tools to use in dealing with difficult dilemmas. A concentration on developing such standards provides individuals and the group with an understanding of the difference between right and wrong and of the rationale for making ethical decisions. And, this process of giving serious thought to ethical issues also helps promote moral courage and helps establish how moral courage plays a part in decision-making

Ethics is Two Things

The word, "ethics," refers to well-based standards of right and wrong that prescribe what human rights ought to do. Ethics, for example, refers to those standards that impose the reasonable obligations to refrain from rape, stealing, murder, assault, slander, and fraud. Ethical standards also include those that enjoin virtues of honesty, compassion, and loyalty.

And, ethical standards include standards relating to rights, such as the right to life, the right to freedom from injury, and the right to privacy. Such standards are adequate standards of ethics because they are supported by consistent and well-founded reasons.

Secondly, ethics refers to the study and development of one's ethical standards. Feelings, laws, and social norms can deviate from what is ethical. So it is necessary to constantly examine one's standards to ensure that they are reasonable and well founded.

Ethics also means, then, the continuous efforts of studying our own moral beliefs and our moral conduct, and striving to ensure that we, and the institutions we help to shape, live up to standards that are reasonable and solidly-based.

Function of Code of Ethics

Members of a profession encourage each other to observe and practice high ethical standards by developing and embracing a code of ethics. Most such codes identify some core concepts. Once developed, a code then serve as a collective recognition by members of a profession of its responsibilities and creates an environment in which ethical behavior is the norm.

Whether the code becomes a framed document on an office wall, or a type of conscience-compass which is internalized, once embraced, the code of ethics serves as a guide or reminder in specific situations and can indicate to others that the profession is seriously concerned with responsible, professional conduct.

The process of developing and modifying a code of ethics can be valuable for a profession, especially since it can serve as an educational tool, providing a focal point for discussion in classes and professional meetings. [7]

Ethical Decision Making

Ethics or morality poses questions about how we ought to act and how we should live, and for a school administrator, guides the day-by-day decision-making associated with being a leader. It asks, "According to what standards are these actions right or wrong?" It asks, "What character traits—like honesty, compassion, fairness—are necessary to live a truly human life?" It also asks, "What concerns or groups do we usually minimize or ignore?"

Decision-making is an integral part of the administrator's daily life. Each such decision should be approached in a five-step process:

1. Recognize a Moral Issue,
2. Get the Facts,
3. Evaluate the Alternative Actions,
4. Make a Decision, and,
5. Act — Then, Reflect on the Decision Later.

---

[7] Center for the Study of Ethics in Professions (CSEP)

Approaching Ethics

Taking the initial step in an ethics-related action can be considered in a variety of ways—the virtue approach, the utilitarian approach, the rights approach, the fairness (or justice) approach, or the common good approach.

The Virtue Approach—Focuses on attitudes, dispositions, or character traits that enable us to be and to act in ways that develop our human potential. Examples are honesty, courage, faithfulness, trustworthiness, and integrity. The principle states: "What is ethical is what develops moral virtues in ourselves and our communities."

The Common Good Approach—Presents a vision of society as a community whose members are joined in a shared pursuit of values and goals they hold in common. The community is comprised of individuals whose own good is inextricably bound to the good of the whole. The principle states: "What is ethical is what advances the common good."

The Fairness (or Justice) Approach— Focuses on how fairly or unfairly our actions distribute and burdens among the members of a group. Fairness requires consistency in the way people are treated. The principle states: "Treat people the same unless there are morally relevant differences between them."

The Rights Approach— Identifies certain interests or activities that our behavior must respect, especially those areas of our lives that are of such value to us that they merit protection from others. Each person has a fundamental right to be respected and treated as a free and equal rational person capable of making his or her own decisions. This implies other rights (e.g., privacy free consent, freedom of conscience, etc.) that must be protected. The principle states: "An action or policy is morally right only if those persons affected by the decision are not used merely as instruments for advancing some goal, but are fully informed and treated only as they have freely and knowingly consented to be treated."

The Utilitarian Approach— Focuses on the consequences that actions or policies have on the well being ("utility") of all persons directly or indirectly affected by the action or policy. The principle states: "Of any two actions, the most ethical one will produce the greatest balance of benefits over harms."[8]

---

[8] Velasquez, Manuel; Andre, Claire; Shanks, Thomas, and Meyer, Michael J. *Approaching Ethics*. Markkula Center of Applied Ethics, Santa Clara, 2014.

CHAPTER FOUR

Immeasurable Asset —

The trust that all the students, parents, employees and others in the community place in a school district and the professional educators and all the employees of the school district is an asset of immeasurable value. Each staff member has a personal responsibility to guard this trust, maintain it, and strengthen it—especially so for the school administrators who are chosen to lead and serve.

Every school leader has a circle of influence. Even though those circles may vary in size, every administrator has the capacity, even power, to impact others. That impact could be for good or for bad, depending on the convictions of the leader.

School administrators are highly visible in virtually every aspect of their life and work. Whether at school, in the business community, in the social arena, in civic organizations, at church, at home, in other communities, at the State House, in the stadium at an athletic event, or anywhere in the world, the administrator's life is on display. Each act is observed by all who have eyes to see and each spoken word is listened to by those who have ears to hear. Words, attitudes and actions, individually or collectively, send messages that impact others.

The convictions that are embraced by an administrator guide the leader's behavior, whatever the circumstances or environment. The opportunity to compromise is always present. A firm belief that one should always behave in an ethical manner, maintaining integrity under all conditions, will strengthen ones ability to avoid compromising when tempted to do so. There will always be those who may ridicule such values or lifestyle. But respect for "taking a stand" will be lessened if one "gives in" by compromising.

A conviction to maintain integrity under all circumstances is an anchor that will hold fast when the winds of controversy blow strongly and when waves of temptation pound hard. Maintaining an unwavering stand that is based on values of honesty, fairness, integrity, ethics, always doing what is right will be a powerful influence on others.

Building "Trust" is critical for an administrator to experience long-term success. Delivering on promises made strengthens trust. Trust is eroded anytime illegal or unethical behavior comes to light. If there are any doubts about what happens when there is a breach of trust, one only needs to recall recent troubles of several major companies in the land and those executives who once led those great corporations. Or, consider the personal damage that has occurred when a few school administrators have violated laws, been convicted of illegal behavior, bringing an end to their careers, embarrassing their families and friends, creating financial and legal difficulties for the school districts they were entrusted to lead.

Leaders need to reflect on an appropriate observation by the author Max Lucado in his small book, *Grace for the*

Moment.[9] The author wrote about "deceit" and the "fall-out" that can come from such behavior.

Lucado's thoughts are appropriate for review as part of this focus on the concepts of "Integrity," "Ethics," "Values" and "Trust" as those concepts apply to those who are school administrators.

What are the results of deceit? What are the results of unethical behavior?

Most people recognize that many of our nation's laws, and many of the values that are embraced by a majority of the population are rooted in some of the nation's religious heritage.

There are many examples of improper behavior by people— and the consequences of that behavior. Unfortunately, almost daily, newspapers contain articles about how people in leadership in the corporate world, in government, and, yes, in education have acted improperly, and the damage that is caused by the unethical, illegal, deceitful actions.

Lucado cites a quotation from the *Book of the Psalms*, and also makes reference to a story of a married couple who lied to their friends at church.

The quote from the Psalms is this —

> *"No one who is dishonest will live in my house;*
> *no liars will stay around me."*
>
> —Psalm 101:7

---

[9] Lucado, Max. *Grace for the Moment.* Nashville: Countryman, a division of Thomas Nelson, Inc., 2000.

After setting the tone with that quotation, Lucado then remarked that: "More than once" he had heard people refer to the story of a man named Ananias and his wife Sapphira (The New Testament story in which a couple conspired to tell a lie about a business transaction and their gift to the church and were "struck dead." because of their deceit) with a nervous chuckle and say, "I'm glad God doesn't still strike people dead for lying."

Then, Lucado reflected, "I'm not so sure he doesn't." He explained:

And, although God may not "strike you dead" for unethical or deceitful behavior as a school administrator, you, your family, your friends, the students, the patrons, your profession, the school district and the entire community all are severely damaged by such behavior.

The trust that all the students, parents, employees and others in the community place in you and in the school district where you are employed is an asset of immeasurable value.

Each of you has a personal responsibility to guard this trust, maintain it, and strengthen it. Hopefully, as you reflect on these things and the contents of this book, you will make a new personal commitment or recommitment to live a life of Trust, Fairness and Integrity.

Chapter Five

"First, Do No Harm"

Among the most respected professions in America are Ministers and Physicians. School Administrators should aspire to have similar respect. Perhaps embracing some similar beliefs and practices would help accomplish such a goal.

"Doing Good" and "Avoiding Harm" are core behavioral standards for both ministers and physicians, as well as for many others, whether because of religious or professional reasons.

The Physicians —

The Medical profession, from its inception as a "profession," has embraced a code of behavior that is commonly known as the *"Hippocratic Oath."* Although there does not appear to be a modern day requirement that all physicians "swear" to that code as part of their legally becoming medical practitioners, most accept modern day versions of the "Oath" as being meaningful and worthy of guiding how patients and families are treated . . . especially the promise, *"Primum non nocere,"* a Latin phrase that means, " First, do not harm."

The *Hippocratic Oath* is one of the oldest binding documents in history. There are various classical and modern versions of the oath. While Hippocrates, the so-called "Father of Medicine," lived in the early Fifth Century B.C., the famous oath that bears his name emerged a century later. No one knows who first penned it. This ancient oath from the Greek has been translated into other languages through the years and has been modified to have greater relevance to citizens of a world that is vastly different from the known world in which Hippocrates lived in the Fifth Century B.C.

The basic ideas of "non-maleficence" and of "beneficence" — the "Do No Harm" and the "Do Good"— are fundamental precepts that those entering the medical profession embrace. They seek to practice the art and science of medicine by not risk causing more harm than good.

The *Hippocratic Oath* is perhaps the most widely known of Greek medical texts. It requires a new physician to swear upon a number of healing gods that he will uphold a number of professional ethical standards. It also strongly binds the student to his teacher and the greater community of physicians with responsibilities similar to that of a family member. In fact, the creation of the Oath may have marked the early stages of medical training to those outside the first families of Hippocratic medicine by requiring strict loyalty.

Over the centuries, the "Oath" has been rewritten often in order to suit the values of different cultures influenced by Greek medicine.

The Ministers —

Those men and women who serve in the Ministerial profession, as a group, are well respected in society in a manner similar to the trust and respect given to the Physicians.

Using one well-established, long-standing religious group — the Methodist denomination — as a representative group, one finds that "the Ministry" also has a code of behavior not unlike that followed by "the Physicians."

In the long and respected history of the Methodist denomination, the person who is acknowledged as the "founding leader" was John Wesley. In his writings, Wesley taught that the denomination was established on three key principles, the first of which was "Do No Harm."

Sound familiar?

Is it any wonder that physicians and ministers, as members of professions, are respected and trusted by the public?

The "General Rules" of United Methodist Christians includes three basic principles, which guide the practice of the spiritual life. John Wesley first proposed these in the mid-1700s as he began a number of small group meetings to encourage, spiritually develop and support his new Methodists. The three principles, each with some detailed instructions, are condensed and paraphrased from the book, *The United Methodist Discipline.*

Ministers are expected to demonstrate with their lives and to teach followers in that denomination to live in accordance with these principles:

First, by "doing no harm," avoiding evil of every kind, especially that which is most generally practiced. Wesley listed many examples, but generally a commitment not "to do to others as we would not they should do unto us," something akin to a reverse statement of the "Golden Rule."

The second principle, "Do Good," was to be accomplished by being kind and merciful, doing good of every possible sort such as giving food to the hungry, clothing to those in need, helping those who are ill, or in prison, or who have spiritual needs.

Wesley's third precept urged people to assemble together, joining with others of similar beliefs, and in a spirit of "Grace" to support, encourage, teach, learn and, in harmony, work together for the betterment and good of the group.

Thus, those who practice in both the Medical Profession and the Ministerial Profession seem to embrace the tenets that they should "Do No Harm" and should "Do Good" in their service and relationships with people. The additional guideline offered by a major group representing the Ministry inferred that we should devote ourselves to the cause, to support and encourage each other, to associate with our peers, individually and with the group, to study as individuals and as a group, to participate both publicly and privately, seeking to be better servants.

Dr. William Cook, Jr., one of the respected educational leaders in the United States, has often stated in his writings and speaking that School Administrators are leaders who see things in a special way, are dedicated to a cause that transcends themselves, live in risk, and "live in a state of Grace.[10]"

That is an interesting thought.

The word, "Grace," has many meanings. In its use in religion, "Grace" is thought of as a gift of God to humankind in Christianity — the infinite love, mercy, favor and goodwill shown to humankind by God. Perhaps Dr. Cook was implying that school administrators are given love, mercy, favor and

[10] Cook, Speech, "Strategic Planning," Association of California School Administrators (ACSA) Region XI Fall Conference, Bakersfield, October 20, 2012.

goodwill, by the community in which they serve as well as by those who employ them and give oversight to their work.

But, "grace" such as that could be temporary in nature.

The word, "Grace," can be a title used in addressing someone such as a duke, duchess, or archbishop. Or, the word could refer to someone, especially a lady, who demonstrates elegance, beauty and smoothness of form and movement. Grace can also relate to politeness, one who is dignified and demonstrates decent behavior. The word can be used to describe someone who is generous of spirit, who has a capacity to tolerate, accommodate or be forgiving. Certainly, the word, "Grace," can describe a short prayer of thanks, usually before, or sometimes after, a meal.

Perhaps the School Administrators who "live in a state of Grace" are incorporating a little bit of most of those definitions — experiencing love, mercy, favor and goodwill, along with being graceful in behavior, being polite, dignified and behaving decently at all times, and, having a generous spirit, being tolerant and forgiving of people under all conditions — and, certainly giving "Thanks" for the privilege of being in such a responsible role where his or her decisions and actions impact the lives of thousands of citizens, young and old, in the community where chosen to lead and serve.

School administrators, as individuals and as a group, both formally and informally, are acknowledged as being influential leaders. How, then, could school administrators do anything less than those who serve as Physicians and Ministers?

Men and women who serve in those professions embrace these core values: "Do No Harm," "Do Good," and in a "State of Grace" assemble together to support and encourage each other, working privately and publicly to be better servants.

School Administrators should "go and do likewise."

Perhaps, then, those who serve as School Administrators would earn the trust and the respect the public now bequeaths on "the Ministers" and "the Physicians."

CHAPTER SIX

"Golden Rule," "Silver Rule" and Integrity —

The "Golden Rule" Principle

It took centuries for "The Golden Rule" concept to emerge, a fact that attests to its soundness. The concept in a variety of words and phases appears in many writings and many cultures.

Confucius put it in negative form: "What you do not wish done to yourself, do not do to others."

Application of the rule in negative form is easy. It involves no risk. It calls only for restraint. The possibility of error lies only in a failure to invoke the Rule before you act or speak.

But, 500 years after Confucius, the Rule appeared in a positive in the "Sermon on the Mount," and that form has a much deeper implication. The writer of the Book of Matthew recorded the Sermon message given by Jesus of Nazareth in this form:

"Therefore all things whatsoever ye would that men should do to you do ye even so to them: for this is the law and the prophets." (Matthew 7:12)

That is a different twist. What do you want me to do for you? You must have the help of co-workers to succeed. Under the Golden Rule, thus, you must help the other person first. You come second. I do not subscribe to the philosophy in so many current writings about "looking out for number one."

Help your peers. Help your supervisors and others in positions of authority. Do not let yourself be resentful of any credit or reward another peer or one in authority may receive as a result of your work and your ideas. The surest way for that person "on the way to the top" to get there is to pull you up the ladder with him.

Do not overlook the associates with whom you work. By being helpful to your peers and other associates you cement bonds of friendship so that, if you are given recognition or promotion, you will enjoy the good will and support of your associates. But, if perchance, that recognition goes to another, the next best think is that recognition goes to an associate whom you have helped.

Superficially read, or thoughtlessly applied, the Rule may defeat its own purpose. What the Rule really means is this:

> *"Do for the other person what you would*
> *want done for yourself if you were that*
> *other person."*

Thus interpreted, it is the most profound rule ever put together in the field of human relations. But, it will not work unless you think of the other person's interest first.

Service to others, above yourself, is the key.

The "Silver Rule" Principle—

Dr. Kenneth Hancock, a Professor and Assistant Dean at a major university in Oklahoma, offered comments on the reverse version of the principle. Pointing out that "the Christian religion has a definite claim to the 'Golden Rule' in its positive statement form, he explains that the 'Rule' is also called the 'Silver Rule' when stated in a negative way—'Don't do to others what you don't want them to do to you.'"[11]

Professor Hancock pointed out that it is "a rule of reciprocity" of how one should treat others, and observed that the concept is found in every major religion of the world. Its tradition is long and has been a basis of the religious and philosophical idea of how we treat other people, and is found in nearly every ethical tradition.

Ethics and morality are not quite the same concepts. Ethics has to do with the social roles in which a person functions; morality, on the other hand, has to do with what one ought to do as a human beings. Although different, it is difficult at times to keep them totally separate. Professor Hancock observed that a person can be moral according to that person's belief system, but may behave in an unethical manner, and vice versa.

The school administrator, as a caretaker of the public trust, must make decisions that affect many people—students, teachers, staff, parents, and other school district patrons. The administrator's ethical behavior should be based on what he or she would want to happen if someone else was making the decision, reflecting what is in the best interest of the larger

---

[11] Hancock, Kenneth, Electronic communications and interview, March 15, 2014.

group, not the fulfillment of the selfish needs or wants of the decision maker.

While discussing the idea, Professor Hancock asked, "What do people want from a leader?" He suggested that "honesty" and "integrity" would probably be at the top of the list. All those who are under the broad umbrella of "followers" expect a leader to tell them the truth and to do the right thing at all times, even when people are not around to see what the leader is doing. The people want to be able to trust the leader in his/her words and actions when doing the work of the people. To do so is ethical. To not do is unethical.[12]

Intellectual Honesty—

The principle of "Intellectual Honesty" is discussed at length in a fascinating little book, *If I Were Twenty-One*, written almost a Century ago. The author was William Maxwell, a veteran business executive, who desired to pass on a few tips for persons just beginning their careers. Maxwell introduced the "Intellectual Honesty" principle with this point:

> *"When you go out into the world you will be confronted with the dishonesty of honest men."*[13]

He explained that some otherwise honest men—when they think it is important in order to sustain their own selfish interests—will often try to persuade themselves into believing

---

[12] Hancock, Kenneth. Electronic communications, interview, March 15, 2014.
[13] Maxwell, William. *If I Were Twenty-One: Tips from a Business Veteran*. Philadelphia and London: J, B. Lippincott, 1917.

what they know is not true. In polite circles, it is called, "rationalization," a kind of dishonesty that fools nobody but himself or herself. Most of us are more or less guilty of it at times.

We all know there are two sides to every coin. But, as long as we refuse to see anything but our side of the coin, and as long as the other fellow refuses to see anything but his side of the coin, we are led into useless controversy that advances the interest of no one. But, we can reach that impasse only because we have already deceived ourselves into believing that there is but one side of this particular coin—our side.

Shakespeare gives the solution:

> *"This above all: to thine ownself be true,*
> *And it must follow, as the night the day,*
> *Thou canst not then be false to any man."*
> *—Hamlet*

What should one do? Become honest—first with oneself— and take a good, long look at the other side of the coin. Just as there are two sides to every coin, so also are there two sides to every controversy. And one side may be just as right as the other when all the facts on both sides of the coin are fully understood.

There will be times when you will be criticized for your conduct or your work. If you were to allow your natural impulse to take over, you would be on the defensive, as if responding to a personal affront, attempting to justify every mistake or difference of view. If you were guided by intellectual honesty, though, you would welcome the criticism as an opportunity to receive the instruction that may be needed in order to accomplish the main objective.

Let the chips "fall where they may." Join hands with superiors and associates in probing for the objective truth. Get the job done . . . and done right.

There is never any conflict between the path to success and the finer instincts within us. Success is based upon objective truth and utter honesty with self and with others.

If you will honestly work on the task at hand as hard as you can—and long enough to get it done right; and, if you will apply the "Golden Rule" with relentless honesty with self, eventual success will occur.

That is the wisdom of the ages.

CHAPTER SEVEN

Encouraging Others

A single strand of twine or rope has a level of strength all alone. But, when the tensile strength of a stretch reaches a certain level, that single strand breaks. Scientists relate studies, though, to prove that as few as three strands, even loosely held together, are more than three-times the strength of one strand. And, if those strands are wrapped or braided, the strength of the three stands is significantly increased.

Let us take the concept from one of Physics and apply to People.

Remember the suggestion introduced earlier that administrators might be wise to embrace the tenets — "First, Do No Harm," then, "Do Good"? The third principle was one that encouraged administrators to assemble together, and in a spirit of grace to support, encourage, teach, learn and in harmony, work together for the betterment of the group.

What exactly does *encourage* mean?

This word means to give somebody hope, confidence; to urge somebody in a helpful way to do or be something; to assist something to occur; to call to one's side; to help, console, or strengthen; or to instill courage in another person.[14]

Many school administrators freely give of themselves to others. They enjoy making new friends and being with associates. They simply "love people" and others enjoy being around them because they are always ready with an encouraging word.

Some administrators, though, consider themselves self-sufficient. They remain focused on themselves and their own needs, being viewed as a "loner." Living or working in isolation isn't wise. The life of a school administrator should be one of relationships. One of the powerful aspects of being involved with others—being part of a "community"—is that those friends and associates are able to give and receive encouragement.

Administrators need to be a part of a larger support group, one in which each participant is strengthened by being part of a "body" of individuals who have shared interests and often some common goals. The "principle" of "togetherness" when two or three or more are bound together, the "strength" is far greater than if three attempt to work individually for resolution.

When one, or a small group, face a critical need, seemingly all alone in the attempt to avert being severely damaged, those persons need to know that there is a "body" of support on which they can depend.

---

[14] Morris, William (Ed.). *The American Heritage Dictionary of the English Language.* New York, American Heritage Publishing Company; and, encourage. 2014. Merriam-Webster.com. Retrieved September 17, 2014, from http://www.merriam-webster.com/dictionary.

Just because a particular issue affects only one person or a small group of people, or a few school districts, and doesn't affect us personally, at least in a recognizable way, it is critical that other school administrators share in that concern. Each of us should be willing to speak out on behalf of our associates who are significantly impacted.

Administrators do not serve all alone. There is a need to "stand tall" and "do the right thing" simply because it is "right." Failing to do so could mean that at a time in the future, any one of us might need that group protection.

"Then They Came for Me"

An excellent example of what can happen when the needs of an individual or small group are ignored is shared in the very heart-rending words of a minister who relates, in poetic form, his personal experience during some of the darkest days in recent history.

The oft-quoted message is credited to Martin Niemöller, a prominent Protestant pastor who emerged as an outspoken public foe of Adolf Hitler in the days before and during World War II. His famous "First they came for the Socialists, and I did not speak out . . . " message was given later in life. Despite his ardent nationalism, Niemöller spent the last seven years of Nazi rule in concentration camps. He was one of the earliest Germans to talk publicly about broader complicity in the Holocaust and guilt for what had happened to the Jews.

Here is that message that causes us to think deeply about being concerned for the welfare of our fellowman:

"First they came for the Socialists, and I did not speak out—
  Because I was not a Socialist.

"Then they came for the Trade Unionists, and I did not speak out—
  Because I was not a Trade Unionist.

"Then they came for the Jews, and I did not speak out—
  Because I was not a Jew.

"Then they came for me—
  and there was no one left to speak for me."[15]

The quotation is from Niemöller's many lectures during the early years following the end of World War II. Different versions of the quotation exist, most likely because Niemöller usually spoke extemporaneously and in a variety of settings in which he referred to many diverse groups. Controversy surrounds the content of the poem. Nonetheless his point was that Germans—in particular, he believed, the leaders of the Protestant churches—had been complicit through their silence in the Nazi imprisonment, persecution, and murder of millions of people.[16]

---

[15] Niemöller, Martin. (1892-1984). Copyright © United States Holocaust Memorial Museum, Washington, D.C.). Retrieved from: http://www.ushmm.org.
[16] Ibid, http://www.ushmm.org.

The lesson learned from Niemöller's experience is that each of us has a moral responsibility to support and encourage those who may be in danger of being harmed.

Think, Say and Do

An example of a group coming together to encourage each person in the group to always do the "right" thing can be found when the members, individually and collectively, embrace some common beliefs or practices—especially concerning "ethical behavior."

In the early 1930s, Herbert J. Taylor, an American businessman, set out to save the Club Aluminum Products distribution company from bankruptcy. He believed himself to be the only person of 250 employees in the company who had hope. His recovery plan started with changing the ethical climate of the company. He explained: "The first job was to set policies for the company that would reflect the high ethics and morals God would want in any business."

If the people who worked for Club Aluminum were to think right, he knew they would do the right thing. Taylor then needed to discover or prepare a simple, easily remembered guide to right conduct—a sort of ethical yardstick—that everyone in the company could memorize and apply to what each one "thought, said and did."

Taylor searched through many books for the answer, but the right phrases didn't surface. In relating the experience, he explained that he then did what many people do when some very special help is needed—he prayed—seeking help from, as he stated, "the One who has all the answers."

After a few moments, Taylor looked up, reached for a card, and wrote down the following twenty-four words that had come to him:

1.   Is it the truth?
2.   Is it fair to all concerned?
3.   Will it build goodwill and better friendships?
4.   Will it be beneficial to all concerned?

Taylor called it, *"The Four-Way Test* of the things we think, say or do." [17]

Many readers recognize the four simple questions as the set of "Beliefs" later adopted by the Rotary Clubs across the land and around the globe that are affiliated with Rotary International. Individual members embrace the four tenets of the Rotary clubs' *"Four Way Test of the Things We Think, Say or Do"* as behavioral standards to be followed in their personal and business lives.

School administrators would be wise to follow a similar set of standards.

---

[17] Taylor, Herbert. "About Us," The 4-Way Test Association, Inc., Retrieved July 2, 2011. Rotary International. Evanston, IL.

CHAPTER EIGHT

Core Principles—
Baker's Dozen, Plus One

In the Medieval Ages there was a period when bakers began cheating the public at such a rate that public outcry reached the ears of several kings. As bread was a daily staple of medieval life, the bakers knew that they could charge a lot of money for minimal portions of their products. As such, kings levied laws against bakers stating that they were to lower their prices and keep honest.

Commonly used now at "donut" shops, the term means that the baker is likely to "toss in an extra one" when a box of tasty pastries is ordered. A more precise explanation is found in the dictionary:

> *"The common term, 'A Baker's Dozen,'— meaning 13 instead of 12—came from the Medieval Age time period. Any baker caught selling less than an even dozen was strictly and harshly punished. As a result, bakers began adding*

one extra loaf to be certain their count would be correct or even over the amount decreed by law."[18]
— *Urban Dictionary*

School administrators, as well as all others in public service—whether in school systems or elsewhere—are personally and professionally obligated to serve the public with honesty and integrity. It is essential that the trust of the public be maintained as the thousands of decisions are made in day-by-day activities of overseeing the operations of a school system.

Building Trust

Trust is strengthened by delivering on our promises. Trust is eroded any time illegal or unethical behavior comes to light. If there are any doubts of these thoughts, just recall recent troubles of several big companies—troubles caused by breach of trust

Central to the standard of ethical conduct is the basic concept that no administrator or other school leader or employee shall have any interest, financial or otherwise, direct or indirect, or engage in any business transaction, or professional activity or incur any obligation of any nature which is in conflict with the discharge of the person's duties in the public interest.

School administrators, in particular, are expected to hold fast to the standards of legal and ethical behavior. What are some of those standards? Every administrator should embrace the following concepts—our *"Baker's Dozen, Plus*

---

[18] Urban Dictionary. 2015.

One" list of 14 recommended guidelines related to how school administrators should live and lead.

Model Standards of Behavior

1. Public service is a public trust, requiring employees to place loyalty to the Constitution of the United States, to the Constitution of the State of Oklahoma, federal and state laws and ethical principles above personal gain.

2. Administrators shall not hold financial interests that conflict with the conscientious performance of duty.

3. Administrators shall not engage in financial transactions using nonpublic information or allow the improper use of such information to further any private interest.

4. Administrators shall not, except as permitted by statutes or regulations, solicit or accept any gift or other item of monetary value from any person or entity seeking official action from, doing business with, or conducting activities regulated by the school district, or whose interests may be substantially affected by the performance or nonperformance of the administrators duties.

5. Administrators shall put forth honest effort in the performance of their duties.

6. Administrators shall not knowingly make unauthorized commitments or promises of any kind purporting to bind the school district.

7. Administrators shall not use public office for private gain.

8. Administrators shall act impartially and not give preferential treatment to any private organization or individual.

9. Administrators shall protect and conserve all public property and shall not use it for other than authorized activities.

10. Administrators shall not engage in outside employment or activities, including seeking or negotiating for employment, that conflict with official school district duties and responsibilities.

11. Administrators shall disclose waste, fraud, abuse, and corruption to appropriate authorities.

12. Administrators shall satisfy in good faith their obligations as citizens, including all financial obligations, especially those—such as Federal, State, or local taxes—that are imposed by law.

13. Administrators shall adhere to all laws and regulations that provide equal opportunity for all Americans regardless of race, color, religion, sex, national origin, age, or handicap.

14. Administrators shall endeavor to avoid any actions creating the appearance that they are violating legal or ethical standards. Whether particular circumstances create an appearance that the law or these standards have been violated shall be determined from the perspective of a reasonable person with knowledge of the relevant facts.

Practice in Daily Life

Let's consider a few examples of how those principles may be observed in an administrator's daily life in a school system.

1. An administrator's loyalties go toward service to the school system rather than personal benefits.
2. School leaders must avoid holding investment in or having other direct involvement with businesses that interact as part of their duty as a school administrator.
3. Information pertaining to the school district shall not be sold or released without proper authorization.
4. Receiving gifts: Coffee, tea, donuts, discounts that are available to the public, greeting cards, plaques of minor intrinsic value, and similar items generally are not considered "gifts" that are inappropriate.
5. Administrators are expected to devote each complete day and week to performance of duties that are directly related to the school district and the position held.
6. Administrators must avoid making obligations on behalf of the school district unless authority has been given to make those commitments.
7. Using information received or developed by the school system, or in the course of duty as an administrator, should not be used to benefit outside financial interests.
8. Administrators must practice a policy of "no special favors" for family, friends or business associates.
9. School equipment and facilities are not "personal" property of an administrator and should be used only for authorized purposes. That includes personal use

of Internet, telephones, computers, copy machines and vehicles.

10. Administrators are under contract with the school district and must not seek or receive compensation from another employer for work performed during the same time period as the school duty.

11. Administrators, and other school staff members, are taxpayers as well as school district employees. Waste and abuse should always be identified, reported and corrected. Appropriate reporting and legal action also must be initiated for detected fraud and corruption at any level.

12. Administrators must model good citizenship, being careful to know and observe all laws and regulations, meeting personal obligations—including paying bills and taxes in timely manner.

13. Awareness of and observance of equal opportunity laws and regulations must become second nature to school administrators. Careful self-evaluation of beliefs and practices is important.

14. Administrators must remain above reproach. Do not engage in any action that you would not want appearing on the front page of tomorrow's newspaper.[19]

The Next Level

This *"Baker's Dozen, Plus One"* set of recommended standards should be embraced by school administrators as a

---

[19] Based, in part, on content of Executive Order 13490, Office of the President (Jan. 21, 2009): *Prescribing Standards of Ethical Conduct for Government Officers and Employees.*

guide for professional behavior—and, perhaps, considered as a "code" for all school district staff members to follow. The concept that "public service is a public trust" is fundamental. All who work in public education are held to high standards, rightly expected to lead by example, and to teach young people that citizens are to be loyal to the Constitution of the United States, to the Constitution of the State of Oklahoma, to federal and state laws and to hold ethical principles above personal gain.

For a school district to be noted as bastion where high ethical practices are the standard will require that the leaders "set the tone" at the top. School staff members, students, parents, the business community and all other observers must see that the ethical standards matter to those in authority.

Chapter Nine

Professional vs. Personal Ethics

Professional and personal responsibility to ethics—are these two different landscapes? The answer is, No!

School administrators, even though selected for their responsible positions through an appointment-contract process, should see themselves as servants of the people and of the people's government. They are not entrusted with the important leadership responsibilities in order to profit themselves, their friends or their families. This is a fundamental concept, one which should guide the activities of a superintendent of schools, as well as other school administrators.

Administrators have been taught how to use sophisticated decision-making procedure models. When time permits, administrators can write down various options, list the pro and con position statements, carefully analyze the best options, develop a plan of evaluation, and then proceed with a decision. The majority of decisions, though, must be made in a matter of minutes. Although the options and analysis procedure may occur, the process is a fast-moving mental review, which is followed by a quick decision.

An internal guidance system which is based on a commitment to legal, ethical and moral values must be in place in the "mind and heart" of the administrator—guiding both professional and personal decisions. When faced with a need to make a decision, whether a "stand-up" situation or a long-range planning process, a wise administrator should have a set of questions permanently inscribed on a mental note pad to help reach a legal and ethical decision.

Questions such as the following are appropriate for that mental note pad:

1. Is the action legal?
2. Is it right?
3. Who will be affected by my actions?
4. Is this action in the best interest of all concerned?
5. Is this treatment something to which I would willingly subject myself?
6. Is there harm being done to anyone without their being able to respond?
7. Is the activity something I am proud of and would publicize as a good trait for others to follow?
8. Does the action I am about to take fit in with the school system's and the community's values?
9. How will I feel afterward?
10. Will my action reflect poorly on the school system?
11. What does what I am about to do, say about me?
12. Is what I am doing something I would feel comfortable explaining to my family, client, friend, husband or wife?

Most administrators, even as children, were given the very sage advice, "Do unto others as you would have done unto you." That oft-used phrase was lifted from the Apostle Matthew's recording of some of the teachings of Jesus, who advised, "So in everything, do to others what you would have them do to you, for this sums up the Law and the Prophets."

This short and simple philosophy is good advice. It just about says it all.

An introductory paragraph in the Oklahoma Political Subdivision Ethics Act contains the clearly-stated provision that the "operation of government be properly conducted so that public officials are independent and impartial and that a public office is not used for private gain other than the remuneration provided by law." In order to protect the public interest in all political subdivisions—schools included—steps must be taken to protect against any conflict of interest and to establish standards for the conduct of elected officials and government employees in situations where conflicts could exist.

Since the work of a superintendent or other school administrator is so time-intensive—not exactly an "eight-to-five" job—separation of the personal life from the professional life often is difficult. The personal-professional lives, at least as viewed by others, become "morphed" into one. What an administrator assumes is a personal activity may be viewed by someone in the community as something performed in an official capacity and representative of the school system.

Administrators and their families live in "glass houses," so to speak. Their private and professional behaviors are observed by and commented on by the community. Functioning under this intense scrutiny can be challenging.

Let's look at a few potholes—personal or outside interest projects—which might be encountered on the administrative roadway and which may invoke some ethical decision-making.

Advocating Issues

A major responsibility of the Superintendent is to keep school district residents fully informed on school district affairs and to encourage open communications between citizens and school leaders at all levels. The Superintendent should set the example for providing prompt, friendly and courteous service to school district patrons—and to students, faculty and staff.

Being able to voice opinions on public issues is something a Superintendent of Schools and other administrators share with other citizens. Care should be taken, though, to be certain that taking a stand on an issue or voicing an opinion on a public matter is handled in a manner that does not conflict with the administrator's performance of official duties. Be careful what and where those personal opinion statements are made.

Use of School-owned Facilities, Equipment, Services

Inappropriate use of school-owned equipment, facilities and materials is something which can easily occur unless the administrator is constantly alert to the potential problem. This action can be something as complex as the use of a school vehicle for a personal vacation trip, the use of a school issued credit card to charge personal purchases, lodging and meals, or can be as simple a matter as using a school letterhead, envelope, and possibly postage to write a letter which is personal and which does not have official school business status.

Following are a few areas of concern:

School stationery is for official school business correspondence, and should not be used for unofficial purposes. Admittedly, the cost is minor—even if school district postage is included. A letter written on official school letterhead implies the school district's endorsement of the content. As an example, a superintendent who uses school district stationery to send a written endorsement of a political candidate is implying that the "organization" concurs in the content of the letter. Separating personal feelings or beliefs from official school position statements is difficult.

Thus, a superintendent or other school leader must make a special effort to avoid any action which has the perception of impropriety. When a superintendent of schools—or other school leader—makes a public statement or takes a public position, there is a perception in the minds of the public that the action or statement is representative of the school system.

Separating public and private life is difficult for an administrator. Be diligent.

Using electronic communication devices has become a way of life for most administrators. The ever-handy "cellular" telephone can be a helpful tool, but this convenient tool also may open the door for some behavior, which could be unethical, or even illegal. A digital-cellular telephone service, which is provided to a school administrator by the school system, should be used for official business purposes. When an administrator uses the school-provided equipment and service to make long-distance calls, which are personal calls, that practice very likely is unethical, if not illegal. The "call time minutes" which are included in the school system's contract for digital-cellular telephone service should be used only for official business.

Similar problems can develop when an administrator makes a personal long-distance telephone call from the office telephone. If circumstances require such personal calls to be made through the school-provided system, a wise administrator should insure that full reimbursement is made to the school district, with an itemized report prepared to document the calls, cost, and reimbursement.

Administrators usually are involved in many civic and community projects and are called on to help with activities which are linked to outside groups. The easy access to equipment, supplies and services can result in misuse of time and other things.

An administrator may be tempted to take time at work to catch up on some non-school projects, such as preparing a newsletter for a neighborhood association or a civic club or perhaps preparing and then reproducing the season's game schedule for the little league team which the administrator coaches.

If staff members in the copy center aren't too busy, an administrator may even ask them to do the printing-copy reproduction work. All that seems innocent enough, but it isn't appropriate. Administrators should use their official time in an honest effort to perform official duties and should not ask or direct staff members to perform activities other than those required for official school purposes.

Furthermore, administrators have a duty to protect and conserve school property (including equipment, supplies and facilities) and may not use school property, or allow its use, for other than authorized purposes.

Outside Employment or Activities

Serving as a school administrator is a full-time work responsibility. A Board of Education and the people of a community have the right to expect the administrator—especially the Superintendent of Schools—to view that assignment as his or her primary "job," and one to which primary mental and physical effort are focused.

Misuse of public time could easily be interpreted as an act of dishonesty.

Operating a side business, running a ranch or farm, spending an inordinate amount of time as a consultant or being involved in outside activities that take time away from the primary mission of being a school administrator simply is not appropriate.

An administrator who wishes to engage in any employment or other outside activities should carefully evaluate whether such activity conflicts in any manner—time included—with his or her official duties. Such activity should be considered only after consultation with and endorsement by the Board of Education.

Following are some outside activities which, although appropriate for administrators, probably should be carefully evaluated and limitations set to insure that the activities do not take the administrator away from his or her primary work for an excessive amount of time:

1. Paid and unpaid service as an expert witness;
2. Participation in professional organizations;
3. Paid and unpaid teaching, speaking, and writing projects;
4. Participation in fund raising activities.

Outside employment and other outside activities of a school administrator must meet the test of a basic principle that the participation by the administrator doesn't give even the slightest hint that the use of official position in this activity will result in personal or family private gain or the private gain of any person with whom he has employment or business relations or is otherwise affiliated in a non-school capacity.

In addition, an administrator who wishes to engage in outside employment or other outside activities must comply with applicable state statutes and regulations which prohibit a public official from seeking, accepting or agreeing to receive or accept anything of value in return for being influenced in the performance of an official act or for being induced to take or omit to take any action in violation of official duty.

Teaching, Speaking and Writing

Teaching, speaking and writing activities often help administrators keep their skills honed and also may be viewed by some as a means of supplementing an administrator's income at the same time.

Is there any problem with such activity?

If the administrator plans to accept compensation (including travel expenses for transportation and lodging) for these activities, then some caution is urged.

Some teaching, speaking and writing activities are performed without compensation, and often are directly or indirectly related to the administrator's specific job and to the school system. The issue of ethics enters the picture if those activities are performed, fully or partially, during the time the administrator is "on the job" and when additional compensation is received.

A school administrator should not accept compensation from any source other than the school system for teaching, speaking or writing that relates to the administrator's official duties. One might define "official" according to these guidelines:

1. The activity is undertaken as part of the employee's contracted, administrative capacity duties;

2. The circumstances indicate that the invitation to engage in the activity was extended to the administrator primarily because of his or her official position rather than his or her expertise on the particular subject matter;

3. The invitation to engage in the activity or the offer of compensation for the activity was extended to the employee, directly or indirectly, by a person who has interests that may be affected substantially by performance or nonperformance of the administrator's official duties.

Administrators, though, often are considered to have expertise, which is based on educational background or experience. Invitations are frequently extended for such administrators to teach as adjunct instructors at universities, to speak at professional conferences, or write for professional journals—all because of that experience and education. If compensation is offered, those activities should be limited to times, which do not conflict with the administrator's contracted hours or days. Many administrators are provided by contract a set number of days, which may be used for service as a consultant or for other teaching, speaking or writing opportunities. If available, those days should be used when the administrator is to be compensated for the work. If a contract doesn't contain a provision for such release time, an administrator should use personal vacation days or request leave without pay when involved in such activities for which additional compensation is received.

Compensation takes many forms. In addition to there being an actual direct receipt of compensation by the administrator, that term also should include compensation paid to another person, including a charitable organization which is designated by the administrator, or any compensation which is paid with the administrator's knowledge and acquiescence to a parent, sibling, spouse, child, or dependent relative.

Political Involvement

Political and lobbying activity can take many forms. Some are obvious, like making contributions to political candidates, political parties or Political Action Committees (PACs). Others are less apparent, paying for lunch with a public official, allowing an officeholder or candidates to use school conference room for a political event, or simply meeting with an officeholder to discuss some legislation impacting education.

Candidates for political office actively seek the support of school administrators and often ask administrators to give endorsements to candidates or to assist in raising funds for political campaigns. School administrators are highly visible in a community, and separating personal life from professional life often is very difficult—especially when related to political campaigns. To the average citizen, the private "Citizen James Smith" is one and the same as the community's "Superintendent James Smith." The private and professional lives are closely intertwined.

Administrators must exercise extreme caution in the public endorsement of candidates for political office—at any level.

Administrators, as well as other school staff members, are encouraged to engage in the political process using their own time and resources, beginning with registration to vote and voting in all elections. Volunteering personal time to support candidates and participating in political party activities is appropriate.

School district resources, though, should not be used for personal political activities. Those resources include, but are not limited to, computers, copiers, telephones, and school facilities.

Voluntarily contributing personal monies to candidates, political parties, or ballot measures are permitted; however, the administrator, or other school staff, must not suggest or imply that the action is on behalf of the school district.

Lobbying, or other political activities are highly regulated by Federal and state laws and regulations. Administrators must insure that every applicable law is observed. The laws are designed to protect the integrity of the democratic process. If violated, they can have significant consequences for the school district and the individual.

School administrators must be aware of the laws and regulations, and pay attention to restrictions on monetary contributions to candidates, elected officials and PACs. Those regulations also apply to non-monetary or "in-kind" contributions to candidates, elected officials, political parties and PACs.

Political Endorsements

The endorsement of an individual candidate for a school board position is certainly unethical, but also can be extremely dangerous from a professional employment basis. The wise superintendent should treat each school board candidate in a friendly, unbiased manner, recognizing that whomever is elected must be assimilated into the elected body of the Board of Education in a manner which best serves the school system and the community.

While on the political endorsement topic, be careful that some enterprising campaign worker doesn't place a candidate's campaign bumper sticker on the superintendent's car, or some other school vehicle such as a school bus. It does occur. The Attorney General of Oklahoma cautions that doing so is a serious violation of the Oklahoma Constitution which prohibits any person from displaying on a vehicle owned by a public school district a bumper sticker promoting a candidate for political office. *(AG Op. No. 86-22, October 28, 1986)*

Whatever the political involvement, the administrator must make sure the effort is on "your own time." Defining that personal time is a bit more difficult for the superintendent of schools.

Political Fund Raising

The ethical issues are even greater when extended to fund raising for a political party, candidate for partisan political office, or being part of a partisan political group's activities. Such involvement raises some ethical issues for the administrator.

Using the position of leadership in a school system as a power base to contact other school staff members to solicit, accept, or receive political contributions should be avoided. And, the administrator must insure that other school employees do not get involved in political fund raising at school or on school time. The Oklahoma Statute is quite clear on this matter. The law provides the following:

"A person shall not use or authorize the use of public funds, property, or time, to participate or assist in the organization of or preparation for a fund raiser for a campaign or in any solicitation of funds for or against a candidate for state office or a ballot measure."

Just be careful. The legal, ethical way: "Don't do it on the job or at school!"

Conferences and Other Events

When an administrator is participating in an official capacity as a speaker or panel member at a conference or other professional event, the acceptance of free attendance, including a meal or refreshments, on the day of his/her presentation, is appropriate and should not be considered a breach of ethics. The administrator's participation in the event on that day is viewed as a customary and necessary part of his/her duties and should not be considered a gift to him/her or the school or organization.

Widely Attended Gatherings

When it is determined that an administrator's attendance at all or an appropriate part of an event is in the interest of the school system or organization because it will further the school or organization programs and operations, an administrator may accept an unsolicited gift of free attendance from the sponsor of the event without that donated conference fee being considered a breach of ethics—if the event is found to be a widely attended gathering. A gathering is widely attended if a large number of people with mutual interests are expected to attend and the event is open to members from throughout a given industry or profession.

A determination that an employee's attendance at a widely attended gathering is in the interest of the school or organization should be documented in writing and placed on file for future reference, if ever needed. If the person extending the invitation has interests that may be substantially affected by the performance or nonperformance of an administrator's official duties, or is an association or organization the majority of whose members have such interests, the determination and written documentation is especially important.

Social Invitations

Administrators often find themselves invited to a variety of social activities. Is such attendance and the acceptance of food and refreshments at the event a breach of ethical behavior? There may be exceptional situations, but usually an administrator may accept food, inexpensive refreshments—not including travel and lodging—at a social event attended by several people where the invitation is from someone who is not a prohibited source and when no fee is charged to anyone in attendance.

Gift Giving and Receiving

The giving and receiving of gifts and other gratuities can present some real challenges to the school administrator.

Gifts to the School or Organization

As a general standard, school administrators or other representatives of a school system should not accept or solicit personal gifts. Offered gifts should be politely and respectfully declined. In some circumstances, it may not be possible to return a gift without causing embarrassment, or the gift may be a consumable item, which cannot be returned easily. In such cases, school leaders should rely on sound conservative judgment.

Policies should be developed to guide administrators about how to deal with offers of gifts and bequests, which are offered to the school system. The school system should be able to accept gifts and bequests in certain circumstances. The authority to receive, properly acknowledge and account for such gifts should be carefully defined in school policies, developed with the guidance of the school administrator and adopted by the Board of Education. The policy should identify who within the school system or organization has the authority to act on behalf of the school or organization to accept gifts, and under what conditions.

In order to obtain approval to accept a gift to the school or organization, a written request should be submitted. That request should be reviewed by the Board of Education. The request should include a Gift Donation Form, completed by the donor, and with the form used to document for inventory or deposit purposes the transaction.

Gifts from Employees

Gifts from school, department or organization employees will generally not be accepted—with a possible exception of a group celebration of a significant honor, promotion, retirement or some similar event. The wise administrator should make that policy known in advance to staff members and should issue a reminder before approaching birthdays, anniversaries or special holidays.

Employees should not solicit a gift or encourage the solicitation of a gift for other employees in the school or organization unless the chief administrator has approved it. Such approval should be limited to significant events such as an honor, promotion or retirement.

Nominating a school or organization program for an award is not considered soliciting a gift.

Gifts from Outside Sources

An administrator must not solicit or accept a gift given because of his or her official position or from a prohibited source to include anyone who:

1. Has or seeks official action or business with the school system.
2. Is regulated by the school system.
3. Has interests that may be substantially affected by the performance of an employee's official duties; or
4. Is an organization composed mainly of persons described above.

Items such as publicly available discounts and prizes, commercial loans, food not part of a meal such as coffee and doughnuts, and items of little value such as plaques and greeting cards should not be considered as formal gifts.

Unless the frequency of the acceptance of gifts would appear to be improper, a school employee may accept gifts in accordance with these suggested guidelines:

1. Nominal gifts based on a personal relationship when it is clear that the motivation is not his/her official position.
2. Gifts of $20 or less per occasion, not to exceed $50 in a year from one source.
3. Discounts and similar benefits offered to a broad class, including a broad class of (school/organization) employees.

4. Most genuine awards and honorary degrees, although in some cases an employee will need a formal determination.

5. Free attendance, food, refreshments and materials provided at a conference or widely attended gathering or certain other social events which an employee attends with approval in his/her official capacity.

6. Gifts based on a non-school, outside business relationship. An administrator or other school employee should graciously return gifts not meeting the exceptions. Perishable items should be given to charity or shared by the office staff, with approval of the chief administrator.

CHAPTER TEN

Ethics in Personnel Matters

Human resources-personnel functions are among the essential management activities to which the superintendent of schools must devote a significant amount of time and attention. This is a critical area, and one that can be fraught with risks.

Taking care of the human resources functions of the superintendent of schools requires careful planning and oversight. Faced with the variety of personnel activities—recruiting, appraisal and selection, orientation, staff development, legal aspects, employment justice, compensation, bargaining and others—the superintendent must share authority with other administrators.

Primarily dependent upon the size of a school district, the personnel functions may be vested in a Personnel Department, be a responsibility resting solely or primarily with the Business Department, or have its needs split among a variety of school departments.

Finding and keeping qualified people becomes a priority. It is therefore essential that the best people available candidates be utilized in the best manner possible in positions designed to meet the total needs of the school system. This process can present challenges for the superintendent and staff.

Ethical issues must be considered both from the personal standpoint of how the superintendent or other administrator functions while employing and supervising others; and, how these administrators act concerning their own contract with the school system.

Loyalty

The virtue of loyalty ought to be an incentive for responsible administrators and administration.

An administrator who wants to "play" honorably in the world of work needs professionalism, money, and loyalty. Loyalty among people remains a relevant value in the contemporary world of work. Loyalty is the quality of being loyal, of faithfulness to commitments, to obligations, to the school system, adherence to a leader, or to a cause.

Loyalty is very much part of the human social condition. As our concept of loyalty develops over a lifetime, it becomes subject to judgment and justification: the kind of loyalties— personal and professional, the nature of the interactions therein, the objects of loyalty—people and purposes. Reason and emotion should enter in to both our judgments and our justifications.

Few areas of school administration need greater attention to the concept of loyalty than the human resources management arena where loyalty is a key factor in the ethical behavior of administrators who deal with personnel issues. Consider a few examples.

Recruiting a Neighbor's Staff

If a modern new set of Commandments were being brought down from Mount Sinai by Moses during these days, there might me an amendment to the existing tenth commandment related to "coveting."

Exodus 20:17 gives this commandment:

> *"You shall not covet your neighbor's house. You shall not covet your neighbor's wife, or his manservant or maidservant, his ox or donkey, or <u>anything</u> that belongs to your neighbor."*

If an amendment were offered today, the changed wording might read, "or anything—including teachers and staff that belong to your neighbor, especially during the weeks before the start of a new school year."

When the minutes on the clock count down toward the opening day of school, and critical vacancies still exist, there is the temptation to actively recruit staff from neighboring school districts. The recruiting effort flows both directions.

What are some guidelines about how we should treat each other in these personnel recruitment situations?

The ancient Golden Rule, a command based on words of Jesus in the Sermon on the Mount advises: "All things whatsoever ye would that men should do to you, do ye even so to them." Good advice. A slightly different, but parallel version of that concept, is found in the ancient Mosaic Law, which says, "Whatever is hurtful to you, do not do to any other person."

The ethical administrator will treat the neighboring administrator just as he would want to be treated.

Many school districts have adopted policies, which will permit teachers and other staff members to ask and receive a release from contract until the first day of the new fiscal year, July 1 of the new school year. After that date, though, all parties should understand that any request for release from a contract should be considered only when the "losing" school district has been able to employ a qualified, acceptable replacement.

That is a reasonable and ethical plan.

Most administrators do not want to stand in the way of a teacher or an administrator being able to accept an opportunity for professional improvement—a promotion, greater salary, new responsibilities. Thus, reaching an agreement to "release from contract" just as soon as an acceptable successor is located seems to be reasonable.

Ethical behavior is needed on the part of the administrator who is initiating the recruitment effort. Don't go behind your neighbor's back in the effort to employ teachers, administrators or staff. At the very least, a courtesy call should be made to the fellow superintendent of schools to advise him or her that a teacher or staff member is being considered for a position, and to inquire if a release from contract will be considered.

Relations between neighboring school administrators can be easily damaged by unethical employment practices.

Honor Thy Contract

An administrator's employment contract is a written, legal agreement between two parties and should be considered as binding on both parties. Legal documents—employment contracts included—can be enforced by law.

Unfortunately, some school administrators have a tendency to view the employment contract as binding only on the school district. Administrators have been eager to gain the protection of multi-year contracts, yet give little thought to walking away from a contract if faced with an offer of a more attractive job opportunity in another location. Those same individuals are eager to seek a "buy out" by the school district of the balance of the contract if the other party initiates action to end the contract.

A deed, which constitutes an allegation of "breach of contract", can be the action of either party in the agreement. The wise—and ethical—administrator provides advanced notice to the Board of Education of the intent to not extend a contract. And, if there is a desire to seek a release from an existing contract, every effort should be made to meet all the conditions stated in the contract for obtaining such release.

Don't burn bridges. There may be a time when that road needs to be traversed again.

Employment Gratuities and Rewards

The education job market can become very competitive. Potential employees and persons acting in behalf of applicants often seek to exert influence to help gain employment for a relative, friend or associate. Much of that effort is directed toward superintendents or other school administrators who play an important role in the employment process.

At times, though, the normal practices of telephone calls, personal visits, and letters of recommendation are capped by offers of rewards, gratuities or other personal gain in an effort to influence an employment decision. Regardless of how presented or described, all such offers must be rejected. Bribes, rewards, gratuities and other similar offers, which are designed to influence an employment contract, are unlawful—regardless of who offers or receives the benefit.

Among the several sections in the Oklahoma Statutes is the following admonition:

> *"It shall be unlawful and a misdemeanor for any officer or employee of the State Board of Education, a member of a board of education, or other person acting as an agent of the State Board of Education or any board of education, or of any school teacher, or of any person or organization, to pay or accept any fee, commission or remuneration of any kind or character in payment for services rendered in securing positions for teachers in any of the public schools of this state."* (70-6-110)

Other sections of the law outline prohibitions concerning receiving, offering or promising such gratuities or rewards, either as an individual or as an agent. Don't fall into that trap, regardless of how innocent the offer may appear.

Professional Relationships

Superintendents and other key administrators often are contacted by associates in other schools districts with questions about policies and procedures or asked to offer ideas about how best to handle some troubling issue. If advice is shared with an administrator other than the superintendent of the requesting district, that neighboring school superintendent should be made aware of the "advice" or "suggestions" given. Doing so is simply a professional courtesy.

In relationships with colleagues in other school districts and professional associations, it is expected that a school administrator will:

1. Support the actions of a colleague whenever possible, never publicly criticizing or censuring the official;
2. Offer assistance and/or guidance to a colleague when such help is requested or when the need is obvious;
3. Actively support appropriate professional associations aimed at improving school administration and encourage colleagues to do likewise.

Chapter Eleven

Superintendent and Board Relations—

A board of education that enjoys good rapport within itself and with the superintendent of schools is a wondrous thing and a joy to behold. And, a community with such special relationship among its school leaders is fortunate.

In and out of board meetings, effective superintendents and effective board members know their own jobs, and know to get them done. They know, too, what their job "is not." No more would a good board member list "administrative responsibilities" on a job description for a board member than a superintendent would place "policy-making" on the job description for a superintendent of schools.

That mutual understanding of roles is critical to the success of the team. Time or energy of board members should not be wasted on matters that clearly are the responsibility of the administration, and vice versa

There is no more disappointing situation than a public quarrel between a board of education and its chief administrator, with the resulting ill effects upon student, educator and community morale.

If all parties work at it, those quarrels need not occur.

Careful attention to the regular business of the school district, and careful attention to the business agendas that guide each meeting (or should guide each meeting) of the board of education is a major factor in avoiding problems.

The superintendent's job covers a vast array of duties. Serving as the school superintendent is comparable to being the chief executive officer of a vast corporation that offers very many services to a large customer base.

The duties are extensive. A superintendent's responsibilities include the following . . . and more:

- Evaluation
- Planning
- Reporting
- Talent management
- Coordination and management of policies and regulations
- Recommendations for educational programs
- Advisor, counselor, consultant
- Legal, legislative, regulatory specialist
- Financial specialist and good steward
- Et cetera . . . as described by "the King."

"Et cetera, et cetera, et cetera" was a line spoken by King Mongkut of Siam (played by actor Yul Brunner) in the award-winning movie, *The King and I*. That was one of the King's catchphrases when he ran out of words to speak. Most superintendents would agree that the list of duties is almost limitless.

Theoretically, the school board makes policy and the superintendent, as the board's chief executive officer, executes board-mandated policy. From the board, the superintendent receives legal authority and responsibility for designated governance decisions.

But how a school board and superintendent actually operate to lead a school district may depend on their relationship. Sometimes, those relationships become confrontational, with parties becoming aggressive or hostile.

If that occurs, the superintendent should demonstrate his or her leadership skills to restore a productive working relationship and reestablish trust. When the superintendent is perceived as a person of integrity, adhering to high moral and ethical standards, that restoration process is more likely to occur quickly.

Avoiding such controversy should be the goal of a good leader. Embracing a few core concepts should help prevent the confrontations.

Exert Leadership—

While the superintendent must exercise leadership in the educational enterprise, the board must exercise leadership in the community. Board members must be able to explain and defend the decisions they have made. The superintendent must be willing to make recommendations to the board when it is faced with tough decisions; and, both parties must be actively involved in the evaluation of the system.

Delegation of Authority—

Even though boards may understand their policy-making authority, some board members, because of the complexity of the board's business, simply abrogate their decision-making role to the superintendent. This situation is usually based on the assumption that "the superintendent knows all of the answers, so let him do it."

There is a political axiom that says, power flows to those who exercise authority. If the superintendent is forced by default to initiate policy, the board might as well stay home. The superintendent must constantly encourage the board members to be involved in the process.

Understand the Difference—

Superintendents and board members must have a clear understanding of the difference between policy and administrative rule. Perhaps the greatest source of friction between boards and superintendents arises when an understanding cannot be reached in this area. Each party must make a determined effort to understand and respect the position of the other in this all-important aspect of school district operations.

Avoid "hip-pocket" decisions. There may be times when it is necessary to make a split-second decision without historical precedent. If there is a need for a policy, then develop a policy carefully, using two or three board meetings to consider issues and draft wording before final approval is rendered.

Keep Each Other Informed—

Failure to keep others informed can be a deadly action on the part of either party. Nothing disturbs a board of education more than to find that information has been withheld from it on a matter it considers important. By the same token, superintendents quickly lose faith in boards that do not "level with them" on all issues.

The board and superintendent should have agreement that there will be no surprises for each other. There must be complete faith in each other.

Be Open Minded —

The refusal to listen to all the available facts and information can quickly poison the relations between the board and the superintendent. A superintendent must not assume that he or she has the "only answer."

On every matter requiring an action vote by the board of education, the superintendent has a responsibility to prepare a written recommendation, based on the careful analysis by the superintendent and/or staff members concerning the best interests of the district. But, if the board presents new and valid information, if appropriate, the superintendent should be willing to amend the original recommendation. In some cases, the best decision may be to suggest that the matter be referred for action at another meeting.

There is nothing wrong with tabling an item and referring for additional study and action at a later date.

Keep Students in the Center —

Children of the school district should always be kept in the center of the decision-making process. Too often, in seeking to define their relationship, superintendents and board lose sight of the central figures in the educational process, the children of the district. Constant care must be taken that bricks and mortar, dollars and cents, do not become the ends of the educational enterprise rather than the means to the end.

In the consideration of every school board agenda item, or every administrative decision, force yourself to ask, "What is the impact on the students?"

Maintain Impartiality —

Administrators should maintain a reputation of serving equally and impartially all members of the school district governing body—the board of education. Letters, reports, electronic messages sent to one member should be "copied" to other members to avoid any hint of special attention being given to one person.

Superintendents and other school administrators share with other citizens the right and responsibility to vote in all elections. However, in order to maintain effectiveness in a leadership role, during school district elections to choose a member or members of the board of education, a wise superintendent maintains neutrality among candidates for the elected board positions. Information about the school district, the election process, forms and other data, if requested by one candidate, should be provided to all candidates.

Physically and Intellectually Alert—

A superintendent or a board member who refuses to grow in his or her position invites the mistrust of the other party. The board member who considers his or her position a one-night-a-month job simply cannot do justice to the position. The superintendent who considers his or her responsibility ended when he walks out the office door is equally derelict in his or her duty.

The superintendency is a full time occupation. Considering the position anything less than a total commitment is to short-change the school district— the students, the faculty and staff, and the patrons. Spend whatever time is needed to maintain excellent physical and mental fitness in order to be able to properly perform the office to which you have been entrusted.

Scholarship, hard work, attention to business, care and concern for students and school staff members are things that both board members and the superintendent should have as the highest of priorities. If all parties emphasize these traits, a successful relationship can be established and maintained.

Above all, trust must be present. When trust exists, success will follow.

Chapter Twelve

The Business of Procurement

Administrators should always conduct themselves in a manner that will maintain public confidence in themselves, their profession, the local school district, and in the administrator's performance of the public trust. In all behavior, official and personal, the administrator should give the clear impression that he or she cannot be improperly influenced in the performance of official duties.

Living that standard is especially important when an administrator is managing the public's money.

Procurement is the special process of obtaining or acquiring materials and services and is an area that needs careful attention by school administrators in order to walk the ethical "straight and narrow" path. School administrators must make a special effort to protect their own integrity, the integrity of others, and the integrity of the school system while dealing with the public's funds. The commitment to be a "good steward" takes on a special meaning when the public's resources are involved. Few areas in the realm of school administration require such careful attention to ethics, as does that of the relationship between vendors and the schools.

In a field where the vendor generally knows much more about the products than the customer and the sale or acceptance of a proposal is based as much on trust as on any apparent "deal," it is essential that customers have confidence in their vendor's honesty. By the same token, providers of services or products also must have confidence that the buyers of their services also will observe fair, ethical and legal trade practices.

That confidence equates to "having trust" in each other.

What is the best way to build this trust? This can be accomplished by establishing and following a set of standards of ethical conduct for all parties to aspire to in their dealings with their peers, customers, vendors and employees.

Because personnel who are involved in the procurement function are in a position to provide or withhold substantial rewards for suppliers who serve the company, school or organization, and because they constantly operate under pressures from conflicting sources, they must have a highly developed sense of professional ethics to resist these pressures and to serve the company, school or organization in an honorable way.

Ethics and Trust are standards that both buyers and suppliers must observe. Those standards for behavior often are clearly specified in professional Codes of Ethics that have been officially adopted by various professional associations.

Observing a Code of Ethics

Why have a code of ethics? Codes of ethics are controversial documents. Some writers have suggested that codes of professional ethics are pointless and unnecessary.

Many others believe that codes are useful and important, but disagree about why.

At one end of the spectrum is the argument that codes of ethics serve no good purpose whatever. Those individuals feel that ethics should be open-ended and reflective, and that relying on a code of ethics is to confuse ethics with law. They also assert that it is mistaken to assume that there is a special ethics for professionals, which is separate from the ethics of ordinary human beings within a moral society.[20]

Supporters of that position suggest that professionals, thus, have no special rights or duties separate from their rights and duties as moral persons, and therefore codes of ethics are pointless and possibly pernicious.

A different sort of attack on the usefulness of codes of ethics comes from those who acknowledge that codes of ethics do have some sociological value. Luegenbiehl writes, "The adoption of a code is significant for the professionalization of an occupational group, because it is one of the external hallmarks testifying to the claim that the group recognizes an obligation to society that transcends mere economic self-interest."[21]

But he believes that ultimately codes of ethics create moral problems rather than helping to resolve them. Those who hold to that position feel that practicing professionals rarely turn to their codes of ethics for guidance, and that the guidelines within the codes sometimes seem internally inconsistent. A

[20] Ladd, John. *Introduction. Codes of Ethics Online,* Center for the Study of Ethics in Professions (CSEP): http://csep.iit.edu/codes/coe, 1999.
[21] Luegenbiehl, Heinz C. "Codes of Ethics and the Moral Education of Engineers," *Business and Professional Ethics Journal.* 1983.

concern with that position is that implementation of a code of ethics may be in conflict with the moral autonomy which is expected of individuals.

Administrators should understand that codes of ethics are not recipes for decision-making, but are expressions of ethical considerations to bear in mind. These guidelines form an ethical framework rather than give specific solutions to problems.

With that in mind, consider some of the issues that administrators face in coordinating the procurement practices in a school system—the bidding, buying and borrowing functions.

Bidding and Buying

An administrator who seeks to direct purchases to certain favored vendors or who seeks to circumvent a competitive bidding process—for whatever reason—is perceived as breaching the public's trust. The bidding process, both from the standpoint of the school system as the buyer and from the bidders who seek to be vendors to the school system, must be conducted with the highest of ethical standards.

The superintendent of schools must insure that all purchasing activities are conducted impartially so as to assure fair competitive participation in the school system purchasing and contract award activities by responsible vendors and contractors. Moreover, administrators must conduct themselves in such a manner as to foster public confidence in the integrity of the school system's procurement process.

There are those who may want to manipulate the bidding process, even to the point of asking a bidder to lower his bid to that which has been submitted by another potential vendor or contractor in order to give favor to a vendor. Even if the bids being considered may not be at the level which fall under the required sealed bid statutes, such behavior is unethical and probably illegal. Don't do it!

Bidders have a right to expect that their bids will be taken as a serious offer to do business, not as a means of manipulating a competitor. And, such behavior by an administrator and a vendor starts a bidding-buying process, which is built on the wrong kind of relationship—one in which each knows the other is willing to do some shady dealing. When something goes wrong and defenses go up, things are more likely to turn sour if each already has reason to distrust the other.

The entire procurement process must be founded on a high level of trust.

Thus, the superintendent must see that ethical standards, such as the following, be observed:

Procurement Ethics—Some General Standards

It is a serious breach of the public trust to subvert the purchasing process by directing purchases to certain favored vendors, or to tamper with the competitive bidding process, whether it's done for kickbacks, friendship or any other reason.

Here are some General Ethical Standards related to bidding, buying and borrowing:

1. It shall be a breach of ethics to attempt to realize personal gain through employment by any conduct inconsistent with the proper discharge of the employee's duties.

2. It shall be a breach of ethics to attempt to influence any employee to breach the standards of ethical conduct set forth in this code.

3. It shall be a breach of ethics for any employee to participate directly or indirectly in procurement when the employee knows that:

    a. the employee or any member of the employee's immediate family has a financial interest pertaining to the procurement;

    b. a business or organization in which the employee, or any member of the employee's immediate family, has a financial interest pertaining to the procurement; or

    c. any other person, business or organization with which the employee or any member of the employee's immediate family is negotiating or has an arrangement concerning prospective employment is involved in the procurement.

4. Gratuities. It shall be a breach of ethics to offer, give or agree to give any employee or former employee, or for any employee or former employee to solicit, demand, accept or agree to accept from another person, a gratuity or an offer of employment in connection with any decision, approval, disapproval, recommendation, preparation of any part of a program requirement or purchase request, influencing the content of any specification or procurement standard, rendering of advice, investigation, auditing, or in any other advisory capacity in any proceeding or application, request

for ruling, determination, claim or controversy, or other particular matter pertaining to any program requirement or a contract or subcontract, or to any solicitation or proposal therefore pending before this government.

5. Kickbacks. It shall be a breach of ethics for any payment, gratuity or offer of employment to be made by or on behalf of a subcontractor under a contract to the prime contractor or higher tier subcontractor for any contract, or any person associated therewith, as an inducement for the award of a subcontract or order.

6. Contract Clause. The prohibition against gratuities and kickbacks prescribed above shall be conspicuously set forth in every contract and solicitation therefore.

7. It shall be a breach of ethics for any employee or former employee knowingly to use confidential information for actual or anticipated personal gain, or for the actual or anticipated gain of any person.

Concern of Buyers and Sellers

Procurement ethics is a concern of both buyers and sellers—school systems and vendors. Legitimate contractors and vendors have high ethical standards, and most are affiliated with professional organizations, which set forth guidelines, which are surprisingly similar to the guidelines, which professional school administrators observe.

Responsible contractors and vendors make commitments that they will not offer, give, solicit or receive, either directly or indirectly, any contribution to influence the award of a contract by a school system or any public authority. Neither will they offer any gift or other valuable consideration in order to secure work.

Most vendors have the same concerns about maintaining high ethical standards in conducting business with schools—or any other customer. Many organizations, which represent both vendors and suppliers—buyers and sellers—have adopted formal Codes of Ethics which members are expected to observe.

On the following pages are some examples of codes of ethics that have been adopted by various organizations with direct involvement in buying and selling. These example codes can serve as models to guide school administrators, as well as the organizations for which the codes were developed.

National Association of Educational Procurement Code of Ethics

Purchasing professionals must have a highly developed sense of professional ethics to protect their own and their institution's reputation for fair dealing. To strengthen ethical awareness, and to provide guidelines for its Members, NAEP has long promoted a code of ethics.

1. Give first consideration to the objectives and policies of my institution.
2. Strive to obtain the maximum value for each dollar of expenditure.
3. Decline personal gifts or gratuities.

4. Grant all competitive suppliers equal consideration insofar as state or federal statute and institutional policy permit.

5. Conduct business with potential and current suppliers in an atmosphere of good faith, devoid of intentional misrepresentation.

6. Demand honesty in sales representation whether offered through the medium of a verbal or written statement, an advertisement, or a sample of the product.

7. Receive consent of originator of proprietary ideas and designs before using them for competitive purchasing purposes.

8. Make every reasonable effort to negotiate an equitable and mutually agreeable settlement of any controversy with a supplier; and/or be willing to submit any major controversies to arbitration or other third party review, insofar as the established policies of my institution permit.

9. Accord a prompt and courteous reception insofar as conditions permit to all who call on legitimate business missions.

10. Cooperate with trade, industrial and professional associations, and with governmental and private agencies for the purposes of promoting and developing sound business methods.

11. Foster fair, ethical and legal trade practices.

12. Counsel and cooperate with NAEP Members and promote a spirit of unity and a keen interest in professional growth among them.[22]

National Institute for Public Procurement (NIGP) Code of Ethics

The Institute believes, and it is a condition of membership, that the following ethical principles should govern the conduct of every person employed by a public sector procurement or materials management organization:

1. Seeks or accepts a position as head (or employee) only when fully in accord with the professional principles applicable thereto and when confident of possessing the qualifications to serve under those principles to the advantage of the employing organization.

2. Believes in the dignity and worth of the service rendered by the organization, and the societal responsibilities assumed as a trusted public servant.

3. Is governed by the highest ideals of honor and integrity in all public and personal relationships in order to merit the respect and inspire the confidence of the organization and the public being served.

4. Believes that personal aggrandizement or personal profit obtained through misuse of public or personal relationships is dishonest and not tolerable.

---

[22] NIGP: The Institute for Public Procurement. Herndon, VA, http://www.naepnet.org/CodeOfEthics

5. Identifies and eliminates participation of any individual in operational situations where a conflict of interest may be involved.

6. Believes that members of the Institute and its staff should at no time, or under any circumstances, accept directly or indirectly, gifts, gratuities, or other things of value from suppliers, which might influence or appear to influence purchasing decisions.

7. Keeps the governmental organization informed, through appropriate channels, on problems and progress of applicable operations by emphasizing the importance of the facts.

8. Resists encroachment on control of personnel in order to preserve integrity as a professional manager.

9. Handles all personnel matters on a merit basis, and in compliance with applicable laws prohibiting discrimination in employment on the basis of politics, religion, color, national origin, disability, gender, age, pregnancy and other protected characteristics.

10. Seeks or dispenses no personal favors. Handles each administrative problem objectively and empathetically, without discrimination.

11. Subscribes to and supports the professional aims and objectives of NIGP—The Institute for Public Procurement.[23]

---

[23] http://www.nigp.org/eweb/NIGP Code of Ethics

Mail Systems Management Association (MSMA) Vendor Code of Ethics

1. Have a responsibility to conduct myself so that my good faith or integrity shall not be open to question.

2. Will at all times practice and promote the highest possible professional standards.

3. Shall conform to all existing laws and regulations governing the mail and other materials entrusted to my care and disposition and shall never knowingly be party to any illegal or improper activities relative thereto.

4. Shall be prudent in the use of information acquired in the course of my duties. I shall not use information, confidential or otherwise, for any personal gain or in a manner, which would be detrimental to the welfare of others.

5. Shall not accept gifts or gratuities from clients, business associates, or suppliers as inducements to influence any procurement or decisions I shall make.

6. Shall use all reasonable care to obtain factual evidence to support opinions.

7. Shall strive for continuing proficiency and effectiveness in this profession and shall contribute to further research, development and education. It is my professional responsibility to encourage those interested in Mail and Distribution Systems Management and offer assistance, whenever possible, to those who enter the profession and to those already in the profession.

8. Shall practice high ethical standards in dealing with fellow executives and with subordinates as well. Department employees shall be given a pride in the high ethical standards of the department.

9. Have an obligation to my suppliers or vendors: therefore, I shall uphold the highest standards of business ethics, making only reasonable requests from them as I serve my customers.

10. Have an obligation to my employer or employees whose trust I hold: therefore, I shall endeavor to discharge this obligation to the best of my ability, to guard their interest and give counsel wisely.

11. Have an obligation to my customers: therefore, to affirm and retain their confidence, I shall adhere to a policy of truth in business interchange and shall promise only that which can be fulfilled.

12. Accept these obligations as a personal responsibility, I hereby promise that I will abide by the Professional Code of Ethics as declared for Certified Mail and Distribution Systems Suppliers.[24]

Purchasing Function

The purchasing function is considered one of the touchiest jobs in public service. When it is performed fairly and with good management techniques, few people outside the purchasing department concern themselves with the process. Let any questionable practices come to light, however, and the public spotlight—often led by the media—focuses with intensity upon the total organization.

---

[24] http://www.google.com;Mail Systems Management Association Code of Ethics

"Mismanagement in purchasing can throw an entire organization into turmoil and disrepute."[25]

Integrity in Practice

Following are some practices related to the procurement function of administration, which should be carefully observed:

1. Disclosing and Obtaining Information: A present or former employee of, or person acting on behalf of or advising, the school system on a procurement, who has or had access to such information shall not disclose it before the award of the contract to which the information relates. No person shall knowingly obtain such information before the award of the contract to which the information relates

2. Offers of Employment: An official participating personally and substantially in procurement for a contract that is contacted by a bidder regarding employment during the conduct of the procurement shall:

    a. Report the contact to his supervisor in writing; and

    b. Reject the offer; or

    c. Disqualify himself in writing until authorized to resume on grounds that the offeror is no longer a bidder; or all discussions have terminated without an agreement for employment.

---

[25] Wood, Craig R. *Principles of School Business Management*, ASBO International, 1986.

Common Prohibitions

The area of developing contracts must be given careful attention by school administrators since contract documents often are prepared by others, with or without specific instructions from the administrator. Be careful. Following are some recommended common prohibitions related to contracts:

1. Administrators or their representatives must not promise future employment or business opportunities; give or offer money or other gratuity to any individual in connection with procurement of any contract or subcontract; solicit or obtain source selection information from a procurement officer; or accept an offer of future employment, business opportunity, or other gratuity from any prime or subcontractor.

2. In addition, administrators or their representatives must not retain others or be retained to solicit another contract upon an agreement for commission, percentage, brokerage, or contingent fee, except for the retention of bona fide employees or bona fide established commercial selling agencies for the purpose of securing business.

Protecting School's Reputation

Since the reputation of a school district is reflected through the practices of school administrators, and in the procurement function through the activities of the district's purchasing official, a specific Code of Ethics should be developed to guide school administrators in how the school district "does business.

Following is an excellent Code of Ethics that focuses principally on the procurement practices of a school district.

School Business Code of Ethics

1. To regard public service as a sacred trust, giving primary consideration to the interests of the school district and community by which we are employed.
2. To purchase without prejudice, seeking to obtain the maximum benefit for the tax dollar.
3. To avoid unfair and sharp practices (questionable or unethical).
4. To respect our obligations and to require that obligations to our school district be respected.
5. To accord vendor representatives the same courteous treatment we would like to receive.
6. To strive constantly for the improvement of our purchasing methods and of the materials we buy.
7. To counsel and assist fellow purchasing officials in the performance of their duties.
8. To conduct ourselves with fairness and dignity, avoid any conflict of interest, and to demand honesty and truth in buying and selling.
9. To cooperate with all organizations and individuals engaged in enhancing the development of the purchasing profession.
10. To remember that we act as a representative of the school district and to govern those actions accordingly.[26]

---

[26] WASBO Handbook, Wisconsin Association of School Business Officials

CHAPTER THIRTEEN

Electronic Purchasing and Other e-Business Issues

The intent of the innovative concept of electronic purchasing and other e-Business projects is to make purchasing fast, effective and accountable. Paper requisitions, signed approvals, encumbrance orders and invoices fade away in such systems. The revolutionary procurement systems, which are being promoted as the new benchmark for conducting business in both government and private sectors, are very attractive to the computer-savvy school administrators who support "paperless" business practices.

Electronic procurement systems seemingly have the potential for saving significant dollars by eliminating out-dated manual processes and data entry duplication.

An electronic commerce system enables purchasers and suppliers to electronically transact for the purchase and supply of goods and services. The system includes three major hardware and software components: buyer, supplier and bank-administration. To enable suppliers to supply goods and services online and process electronic orders, several software components are used for operating a supplier processor server and a supplier catalog server.

But, be careful.

Can such a system adequately incorporate the important legal and ethical standards that are so critical in school business practices?

Perhaps.

Moving To Electronic Purchasing

Since the shift from an academic network to a functional Internet system in the mid-1980s, transactions between buyers and sellers have moved rapidly from the use of cash and check transactions—the physical realm—to electronic transfers.

The magnitude of this move is anything but insignificant. Online retail transactions doubled from $74 billion in 2004 to $145 billion in 2009. E-commerce manufacturing transactions experienced similar gains, increasing from a little less than $1 trillion in 2004 to $1.8 trillion in 2009; and, by 2011 total e-commerce retail sales increased by 10.9%, despite the economic downturn of that time. The $250 billion mark was expected for 2014 results and even more for 2015.[27]

The Internet is a world of electronic data, where information and ideas can travel at the speed of light. Economically, it is the new way for sellers and buyers to connect, for businesses to communicate with each other, and for companies to show themselves to the world. E-commerce is becoming the mode of choice for transactions of all types in America.

Credit cards, online banking, and other instruments of e-commerce have made it possible for individuals and

---

[27] http://dartmouthbusinessjournal.com/2012/03/transparency-in-the-internet-marketplace-a-move-towards-e-commerce/

businesses to not only transfer larger amounts of currency, but also to do so more rapidly, efficiently, and safely.

That is the nature of business in the corporate world.

School districts, though, operate under a different set of rules. School administrators and boards of education are entrusted with the public's financial resources. What may be "just fine" for the business world may not be appropriate, or even legal, in the school arena.

Many school districts have implemented electronic bidding systems using a variety of software programs. Some have purchased professionally designed programs, such as e-Procurement or Intelisys electronic purchasing systems for schools. Other districts have developed their own systems. The intent, obviously, is to speed up the bidding process, as well as to reduce paper, envelope and mailing expenses.

School electronic business practices have moved to a high level. With that expansion, though, there are both opportunities and problems.

Cooperative Practices

Cooperation in school district purchasing has existed for several years. The electronic procurement concept is becoming more sophisticated and some "best practices" are evolving.

Some states have stepped out quickly. In Colorado, as an example, the large *Mountain Board of Cooperative Educational Services (Mountain BOCES)* provides a wide range of cooperative services and projects—including purchasing options. The desire for cooperative purchasing opportunities was the initial motivation for school districts to join in the collaborative effort. The BOCES serves five Rocky Mountain counties across 8,000 square miles in central Colorado. The organization works in partnership with 10 school districts and the Colorado Mountain College to furnish services that can be more efficiently provided for school districts. The consortium's services include special education, alternative schools and programs, curriculum and staff development, career and technical education, alternative licensure programs, induction, data management and utilization, computer and technology support, cooperative purchasing, and standards and assessment support.

The Mountain BOCES is one of several cooperatives within the *Colorado Board of Cooperative Educational Services (Colorado BOCES) Association.* Nineteen school cooperatives have been formed in Colorado. Many of those, however, were formed for limited purpose projects.

The Colorado cooperatives provide purchasing services through the *Association of Educational Purchasing Agencies (AEPA),* an organization that was formed in 2000 and which the Colorado BOCES joined the following year. The purpose of AEPA is to combine purchasing power to allow all school districts, large and small, the best educational prices available on products and services. There are no membership requirements or fees required to utilize the Colorado BOCES cooperative purchasing contracts.

All biding laws of the 26 member states are covered in the bids issued by the AEPA and the bids have been advertised in at least one major publication in each member state. Each individual state reviews the approved bids and issues contracts to the appropriate vendors, making those contract available through their state cooperatives.

Although Oklahoma is not an AEPA member state, the cooperative purchasing concept can be developed by groups of school districts. That cooperative effort usually involves one school district agreeing to be the purchasing and distributing agent for the cooperating school districts. Some tips for maximizing a purchasing program should include the following:

- Define internal requirements for electronic procurement, including who will be in charge of the program, what is preferred for online ordering, and what supplies should be part of the purchasing process.
- Determine whether there are local companies that will be part of the bidding process, for example, if a firm is a major fundraiser for the school. This might cause a district to bid out materials or services locally, rather than having those be part of a consortium decision.
- Identify whether other organizations in the process are school districts or government agencies or even nonprofit organizations. Sometimes what is suitable for a nonprofit might not mesh well with school district requirements or needs.

Logging On

While school districts are investigating the "how" and "when" to become involved in electronic purchasing, the corporate world is moving very rapidly in that direction. In a research survey conducted by VisaUSA at a National Association of Purchasing Management (NAPM) conference, more than half of the respondents indicated their companies were using Internet-based software for procurement. The respondents were primarily purchasing managers and chief financial officers of corporations.[28] In a 2014 Acquity Group Procurement study, respondents indicated continued increase in online research and buying, with 68 percent of the companies confirming the use of online procurement.[29]

The surveys also found that business-to-business electronic purchasing systems are growing more sophisticated. The process of implementing a new electronic procurement business system involves more than simply introducing a web-based, electronic tool. Significant reforms must take place in purchasing policy and practices to prepare for the introduction of e purchasing. Detailed planning, research, testing and training are essential.

Let's examine a few areas of concern.

Admittedly, the "checks and balances" practices, which are in place in Oklahoma schools—and in most other branches of government—can be a bit inefficient. A myriad of requisition and approval processes are required. Unless the process is carefully managed, delays in the processing of requisitions, invoices and payments can occur.

A question often asked is: Does the manual system result in the school system paying higher prices for goods and services than other comparable organizations because schools may not be able to take advantage of some supplier discounts?

Unless great care is given to obtaining multiple quotations, even on small purchases, group purchases, warehousing,

---

[28] "Businesses Moving Toward Electronic Purchasing." INT Media Group, Incorporated, 2001.

[29] www.acquitygroup.com/docs/.../acquitygroup_2014-b2bstudy.pdf

prompt payment of invoices, and other similar cost-effective practices, the time-honored purchasing policies can result in oversupply, paying too much for goods that did not meet the requirements and other problems.

A basic concept of e-purchasing, thus, is to create a system that fosters better procurement planning, elimination of duplication, and faster delivery of products. The process is a system that emphasizes the purchasing end of the procurement process, not the payment end. By ensuring purchasing practices are right at the beginning of the process, the e-purchasing, in theory, should minimize costly problems such over-supply, over-charging and a lack of quality or suitability of goods on delivery.

A paperless process is envisioned. The system is to cover all stages of procurement—requisition, approval, checking, payment and reconciliation. And, the system should be one which is easy to use and which includes checks and balances to ensure staff acted responsibly.

One of the first tasks that must be accomplished in establishing an electronic purchasing program is that of reforming procurement processes, linking purchasing with planning, and giving less emphasis to price as the overriding consideration and emphasizing value and accountability.

A key point is that of who can approve expenditures. Rather than staff requiring multiple approvals before they can spend money, an electronic purchasing system functions on a concept that purchases are made by staff at various levels of responsibility, rather than with traditional systems which require system-level encumbrance orders, detailed coding, and important accounting steps—most of which are required by statute and regulations.

Decentralization of the purchasing process goes with e-purchasing. But can that decentralization concept comply with statutory and regulatory accounting practices?

With sufficient computer equipment and staff training, most of the procedural concerns probably can be resolved. Still, there are some ethical and legal issues, which must be considered.

The intent of an e-purchasing program is that a school employee can look at an electronic catalog on a computer screen, scan the descriptions and photographs of all common goods and services, glance at the full description and price details, and then simply "click on" an icon on the computer screen and add that item to a personal shopping cart for immediate shipment.

Although convenient and efficient, that process often doesn't comply with requirements related to competitive bidding, pre-approved encumbrance orders, and similar legal requirements, which the school system must honor. Proponents of e-purchasing contend that electronic bidding can be successfully accomplished. A major concern, though, from an ethical standpoint is whether the informality of e-mail bidding will comply with the concept of the security of sealed bids, and whether the electronic communications will open the door for unethical behavior of someone sharing information about a bid, permitting last-minute changes to bid proposals, and other questionable practices.

In the e-purchasing process, steps must be taken to insure that each staff member logs on with their personal ID and password and that all actions are recorded from this point onwards. The concept is one, which depends on the user completing some form of an electronic requisition, which is then automatically sent by e-mail to an authorizing and certifying officer for review and action. Once approved, the order is e-mailed directly to the supplier or printed out for posting or faxing. When the goods arrive, the staff member who made the order acknowledges receipt electronically and electronic transfer pays the supplier automatically, by check, or by school district warrant.

All this may seem attractive, but some doubts remain about whether all legal and ethical standards can be observed.

Ethical Issues

The emergence of the Internet as a tool for communicating with suppliers also has opened up a Pandora's box of issues related to electronic purchasing—as well as other areas which fall under the supervision of school administrators. The informality of communicating with others through e-mail and other electronic transmissions lowers the threshold of awareness of sending information that probably would not be sent in paper form. Many feel that the use of the Internet greatly increases the likelihood of sensitive information being made available through innocence, carelessness or by accident.

Administrators need to be aware of the potential danger of a breach of ethics because of the casual manner in which they and others on staff communicate with suppliers and others through electronic means. Some information, which should be confidential, can be revealed through "off-the-cuff" informal comments of e-mail messages.

In his book *Management: Tasks, Responsibilities, Practices*, Peter Drucker suggests that managers—and that should include school administrators who are both leaders and managers—need to observe as a core ethical principle a concept from the historic *Hippocratic Oath* of the medical profession.

This concept was briefly reviewed in an earlier chapter. Most of us have seen a copy of the oath which often is hidden among the diplomas and certificates on the walls of physicians' offices. The core principle, *"Primum non nocere,"* translates into English as "Above all, do no harm." A more complete portion of the oath translates to "Make a habit of two things—to help, or at least, to do no harm." That is good advice.

This oath certainly applies to the ethical decision-making processes related to electronic purchasing. School administrators who are becoming involved in the world of electronic purchasing need to take special care to avoid possible ethical breaches. What are the additional ethical considerations arising from the introduction of electronic purchasing in schools and other governmental organizations?

In particular, issues such as honesty, equity, confidentiality and conflict of interest all come to light with greater emphasis under any electronic purchasing process.

The ultimate goals of electronic purchasing systems are to reduce costs and increase speed from the time an order is received to the time products or services are delivered to the customer—the school system.

An initial concern is that this new concept introduces a high level of interaction between individuals within the school system who are not traditionally involved in purchasing of materials and services. This interaction can occur in person, in writing, over the telephone, or electronically as an attempt is made to establish and use a so-called "seamless" process— from a customer's desire for something to the actual receipt of the item.

Very likely, legal and ethical standards can become a bit fuzzy because of the greater involvement of individuals who may not know about or understand those legal and ethical issues. Thus, school administrators must establish a series of steps to inform and train all participants about legal and ethical issues—especially the issues of conflict of interest, confidentiality, honesty, and equity—which must be observed in the process of participating in electronic purchasing practices.

The National Association of Purchasing Management (NAPM) recommended that guidelines be developed to focus on ethics in the electronic purchasing process. Two members of the NAPM Ethical Standards Committee, Mark A. Crowder, C.P.M., Olan Mills, Inc. in Chattanooga, Tennessee, and D. Diane Brown, C.P.M., CFPIM, Ernst & Young in Cleveland, Ohio, offered these suggestions:

Seven Steps for Building Ethics Supply Chain Management Model

- Set the ethical standard: You must carry a high degree of personal integrity and "genuineness" into the process or it will fail. Research will lead to better approaches in the future. Nothing can replace your personal commitment to ethical leadership

- Develop mutual goals: The supply chain must have a common set of goals and values in order to succeed. Determine for a key customer or product group what those goals are. This will allow some basis for a shared ethical framework.

- Strategize: Try to project the possible ethical conflicts in a series of "what-if" scenarios. Discuss and negotiate among chain members how best to resolve before the situation actually arises.

- Document: Don't rely on word-of-mouth or "handshake" understandings. This is good common sense, but misunderstandings of large magnitude can and do occur within the open communications of a supply chain relationship—so get it in writing.

- Recognize the competitive environment: Don't put your suppliers in an impossible ethical position. Make sure you agree ahead of time how you will handle jointly developed applications for their products. Can the supplier sell to the open market? Are you willing to pay for exclusivity? These and other concerns need to be addressed.

- Maintain confidentiality in both directions: In open communications, you must be careful to treat your suppliers' confidential information with the same care you expect from them. It's easy to let information slip to other close suppliers who are not involved in the particular project.

- Foster an atmosphere of teamwork: By involving second-and third-tier suppliers, employees, and management in the sourcing process you can build equity into your SCM framework. [30]

Successful Pilot Efforts

A successful electronic purchasing program appears to be in place at San Diego (California) State University. Although California's legal requirements for governmental entities are not identical to Oklahoma's standards, there are some similarities. The pilot effort seems to comply with statutory requirements in that state.

The SDSU program involves contracted services with Science Applications International Corporation (SAIC). The SDSU Intelisys electronic purchasing system was fully operational in late summer, 2000. A unique feature of the system is the ability to process general ledger account numbers in addition to credit card transactions. Authorized users from the university can browse catalogs, create requisitions and get requisition approval—all on-line.

The electronic system permits purchase orders to be automatically generated and sent to suppliers. Receipt entries and electronic invoices are captured for three-way matching. To satisfy accounting requirements, transaction detail containing account numbers, product numbers, descriptions and other information are processed so that accounts receivable can be

---

[30] "Ethical Integrity and the Supply Chain," by Mark A. Crowder, C.P.M., materials manager for Olan Mills, Inc. in Chattanooga, Tennessee, and D. Diane Brown, C.P.M., CFPIM, senior manager for Ernst & Young in Cleveland, Ohio. *National Association of Purchasing Management Newsletter, 1999.*

recharged to customers and to permit the accounts payable department to generate payments to suppliers.

SDSU appears to be one of a handful of entities in the entire nation—private or public sector—which employs true business-to-business e-commerce technology interfaced to a financial accounting system.

The success in this California university is an indication that e-commerce is likely to become operational elsewhere—providing administrators with new legal and ethical challenges.

Commercial Support

Vendors who serve the school market are encouraging school administrators to consider e-commerce programs. In the State of Utah, governmental agencies and others are being introduced to electronic purchasing and related accounting practices through the state's Electronic Purchasing Services, which has been formed to provide state agencies, city and county government, school districts and higher education institutions with an efficient source of office products and other services. EPS and one of the nation's largest business products firms have entered into contract to provide major discounts (more than 50 percent in some cases) on items listed in the office supply firm's national catalog. The program also offers next day delivery as a standard. Electronic Purchasing Services manages the office supplies contract with the supplier to ensure correct pricing, customer service and product availability. Purchases in this system generally utilize a Purchasing Card (P-Card), a customized Visa card, that is designed to supplement or eliminate a variety of processes including petty cash, local check writing, low-value authorizations and small dollar purchase orders. It provides a method of purchasing and payment for small dollar transactions. The P-Card can be used for in-store purchases as well as mail, e-mail, telephone and fax orders. Each card will have pre-established monthly credit limits.

And, school employees who are permitted to use the cards must remember that they are committing school district (public) funds each time the purchasing card is used. This is a responsibility that cannot be taken lightly.

Current Concerns

In Oklahoma, such a non-encumbrance, non-purchase order arrangement most likely would not meet current legal requirements. At the very least, new legislation would be necessary before such a system could be implemented. Even then, such an e-Business roadway is fraught with potholes and the potential for legal and ethical entanglements.

The intent of an e-commerce system for schools and other governmental entities is an end-to-end system. When it comes to buying small-dollar commodities such as office supplies that are bought over and over again, the desire is to allow buyers to shop, make requisitions, get approvals, issue purchase orders, receive invoices and pay for goods, and to do it all online.

For bigger-ticket items and for some services, a basic end-to-end system needs a purchasing department which can post bidding opportunities on its Web site and send e-mail messages of these opportunities to registered vendors. Vendors who are interested in competing for the contract then download the invitation to bid, provide the required proposals and supporting data, and submit a bid—all online. The submitted bids must be collected in the governmental entity's electronic lock-box and automatically tabulated to list the bids from low to high. After such action, the purchasing staff enters in to make the final decision. The successful bidder's name is then posted on the Web site while successful bidders and those who were not successful are notified of the decision by e-mail. A contract is signed with a digital signature and payment is made electronically.

The eventual goal of most e-purchasing programs is to promote the use of individual purchasing cards. A purchasing card should not be permitted to be used for employee travel, lodging, and entertainment expenses. Such use opens the door for mixture of personal expenses with school district expenses. Such is both unethical and illegal.

Administrators will need to give special attention to monitoring records to determine if employee logs of e-purchases match electronic billing invoices. Particular concern is expressed about situations in which items are returned for credit. If cash was received for returned items, care must be taken to insure that the appropriate employee has deposited the cash with the school district rather than retained it for personal use, or entered into some cash transaction using the refund for payment. And, there is a question about whether a "credit" posted on an account is an appropriate way to handle a refund for returned materials.

As indicated earlier, blending e-commerce procedures with state statutes and regulations concerning school finance and accounting is a significant challenge. Key concerns include those of security of information during the bidding process, the danger of not being able to properly encumber funds, the potential for legal and ethical violations through e-mail communications, conflict of interest, confidentiality, honesty, and equity.

Other concerns about e-commerce include these: Does an e-mail message constitute a legal notice for sealed bids? Probably not. Is an electronic lock box secure from those who might access submitted bids and use that data to submit new and lower bid? In this day of master computer "hackers," the security of submitted bids is a concern. Does the date and time information on an e-mail message, which accompanies an attached bid, match the accuracy of a date-time stamp placed on a sealed envelope? Since computer clocks are easily manipulated, the accuracy of e-mail date-time records is a bit questionable.

School leaders also must consider the various costs. Most people are likely to underestimate the cost for school districts and for business and industry to move to online transactions. Apart from the equipment and ongoing maintenance and operational expenses, there are significant costs involved in staff development and re-engineering in both schools and businesses.

Corporate leaders agree that there are long term efficiencies and benefits for industry in moving to online transactions, and, potentially, significant savings for school districts and other governmental entities. However there also are a number of impediments—such as the lack of trust by buyers and vendors, the lack of a rigid legal framework to control e-purchasing activities, and the lack of a badly needed "critical mass" of transactions—all of which may discourage the corporate investments needed for the e-commerce infrastructure to actually make possible the desired online transactions.

Even during the time the Federal government and some state governments have been involved in electronic purchasing, there have been many examples of significant abuse. Appropriate checks and balances have not been developed and implemented

Administrators should enter into e-commerce activity cautiously and with small steps and only in areas where no one can raise legal or ethical questions about action taken. As the late American author Ogden Nash once wrote in one of his witty books, this may be one of those situations which give meaning to the phrase, "You can't get there from here." [31]

Developing Best Practices

School leaders across the land continue to struggle with the e-Business concept, seeking to match the convenience of electronic activities with statutory requirements and other policy and guideline restrictions. In many cases school districts have been able to introduce some flexibility within existing control structures, but many challenges remain. Dr. Patricia (Trish) Williams, Chief Financial Officer of a large urban school district in Oklahoma, spoke of the need to "continually communicate to school district employees about correct school business procedures—even the basic requirement to have a proper encumbrance order obligating

---

[31] Nash, Ogden, *You can't get there from here*. Little, Brown and Company, Boston; 1984.

resources." She described that ongoing process as a "real challenge."[32]

Many school districts permit purchase requests to be created electronically by faculty and staff and then submitted to a principal or director for evaluation and consideration. If, in the opinion of the reviewing official, the request is approved, a purchase requisition is prepared, often electronically, and submitted to the appropriate school business official for preparation of a formal purchase order, if all purchasing criteria are met.

Although there are a few problems to overcome, some school districts send approved purchase orders electronically to vendors as email attachments. That is made possible by use of software applications acquired by those districts. The process is faster than transmission by fax or direct mail, and saves postage costs. A problem encountered by most school districts is that of the frequent changing of email addresses for business firm employees. Keeping business email addresses current seems to be a never-ending challenge for most school business office staff members.

Bidding and procurement system procedures, established by state law, regulations, guidelines and local policies, must be followed. Some of those requirements are difficult to handle properly through electronic means. Requests for Proposals (RFPs) may be published electronically on the Internet. At this point, though, bidders or proposers should be required to submit documents to the school district in hard copy formats in order to accurately meet sealed bid requirements

[32] Williams, Patricia (2015). Electronic communications and interview, March 25, 2015.

and to confirm date and time submission criteria of bidding laws or policies. School districts are required to utilize a competitive bidding process for major contracts above a threshold established in the Oklahoma Competitive Bidding Act. Provisions of that statute must be carefully observed.

Small Purchase Blanket Encumbrances

Many school districts, with appropriate authorization by the boards of education, follow a practice of issuing a limited number of "blanket" encumbrance orders at the beginning of each month. Those encumbrance orders are at designated levels (i.e. $200.00) to certain companies where small purchases are frequently made. Those companies typically are plumbing supply, hardware, auto parts or office supply stores. The purchasing policy for such encumbrances should provide for itemized receipts to be submitted at the end of each month to match and adjust the amount of the encumbrance order.

As far as e-Business is concerned for such purchases, Dr. Williams indicated that the district where she serves as Chief Financial Officer utilizes a limited system for electronic purchases, with a district contract with Office Max for office supplies, and a designated account within the Oklahoma Cost Accounting System (OCAS). She explained that when budget dollars are moved into such a designated account, the system automatically encumbers the amount. An authorized school district employee is then able to purchase (within specific limits) from an on line catalog. This is a carefully controlled structured system that the district requires the vendor to adhere to as part of the contract between the school district and vendor.[33]

Troublesome Issues

One of the pesky problems facing school leaders is the proliferation of relatively inexpensive small technology items and how to identify and track the thousands of individual devices that are purchased with school dollars but "checked out" to students and staff. These devices usually fall below the capitalization threshold of $2,500.00 observed in most school districts; but, because of the threat of theft, school officials must develop a plan to identify and track thousands of the individual devices. Dr. Williams, a large urban school district Chief Financial Officer, said the process was improved in that school district with the development of a tracking system that is installed at the time of purchase. Dr. Williams added, though, "the sheer numbers makes this an ongoing concern."[34]

Mind numbing related problems are developing for school leaders, particularly those charged with financial management. In addition to seeking funds to replace electronic devices, and the control and purchasing issues, there are additional headaches of purchasing "apps" and how to deal with the uncertain movement related to electronic textbooks.

Credit Card Concerns

State laws dealing with credit cards makes on-line purchasing with school credit cards difficult at best.

---

[33] Ibid, Williams
[34] Ibid, Williams

The Oklahoma *School District Transparency Act* became effective in 2010 and requires state website posting by each school districts of a significant amount of financial data. Posting credit card receipts is specifically stated in the law.

That law requires the State Department of Education to maintain a database on its website of school district expenditures that the public may download. The database contains extensive financial information, including credit card statements, and per pupil expenditures as well as budgeted and audited expenditures for each fiscal year. That information must be made available within 120 days after school districts provide the data. School districts that maintain websites must also make such data available on those sites.

Determining if every school district is posting credit card receipts would require extensive research by looking at each school district website, searching for current financial reports under the *School District Transparency Act* link, and looking at the details for credit card transactions.

But, the law requires the posting and those districts that use school district credit cards should be careful to observe that requirement.

Managing what gets charged on credit cards and posting individual card transactions on the local school district website, as well as on the Oklahoma State Department of Education website, could be challenging and time-consuming work for even the most experienced school financial officer. For the present, many school districts have opted not to use school district credit cards, with the possible exception of those cards issued for gasoline purchases for school vehicles.

Will that decision to avoid credit card use continue? Probably not—for a variety of reasons.

The desire is mounting for being able to purchase products through on-line vendors. Many of those vendors refuse to accept purchase orders, electronic or otherwise. They accept credit card payments only. Thus, school districts would be obligated to have school district credit cards to successfully order from those sources.

Software applications for financial accounting programs will be acquired and more school districts will likely begin on-line purchasing using school districts credit cards, even with the burden of additional reporting requirements.

Legal Challenges, Security

Entering into electronic purchasing and other e-Business activities has resulted in school districts making major capital investments in technology, software, electronic infrastructure and training—often without consideration of the short lifespan and the maintenance of the equipment. Incurring long-term debt to finance the purchase of short-life equipment is a questionable use of school resources.

The rush of school district leaders to embrace all forms of technology and to get individual electronic devices in the hands of students, faculty and staff has brought with the movement many troublesome and unanticipated implications. The "perfect storm" of such ill-advised action may be the fiasco of the Los Angeles (California) School District's imprudent $1.3 billion dollar ($1,300,000,000.00) *iPad* project in 2013 that was intended to provide 21st century learning devices to all of the district's 650,000 students.

Hundreds of students initially given *iPads* quickly found ways to bypass security installations, downloading games and freely surfing the Web. Teachers complained they were not properly trained to instruct students with the new technology. And ethical questions about the project were raised after emails were disclosed showing the superintendent of schools had been in communication with vendors before the contract bid process began. The superintendent of schools resigned under pressure.

Allegations have been made about improper financial action related to bidding and conflict of interest issues. The project was cancelled by the school district after the Federal Bureau of Investigation (FBI) seized school records as the result of a federal grand jury investigation. The investigation focused on the former school superintendent's relationship with two major suppliers of equipment and software, as well as the school district's use of long-term obligation construction bond proceeds to purchase devices with short-term life.[35]

Building Ethics Into Policy

Developing policies to guide school district staff members in electronic purchasing or other e-Business functions should reflect high ethical standards. Any employee who is engaged in procurement activities on behalf of the school district should be thoroughly instructed on ethical standards that relate to that process. The "Purchasing Ethics" policies should include the following concepts:

---

[35] http://www.huffingtonpost.com/2014/12/03/fbi-los-angeles-ipad_n_6261988.html

It is a breach of ethics for any employee of the school district to participate directly or indirectly in procurement on behalf of the school district when the employee knows that:

- The employee or any member of the employee's immediate family has an undisclosed financial interest pertaining to the procurement.
- A business or organization in which the employee, or any member of the employee's immediate family, has an undisclosed financial interest pertaining to the procurement.
- Any other person, business or organization with which the employee or any member of the employee's immediate family is negotiating or has an arrangement concerning prospective employment is involved in the procurement.

It is a breach of ethics to offer, give or agree to give any employee of the school district, or for any employee of the school district to solicit, demand, accept or agree to accept from another person, a gratuity or an offer of employment in connection with any decision, approval, disapproval, recommendation, preparation of any part of a program requirement or purchase request, influencing the content, auditing, or in any other advisory capacity in any proceeding or application, request for ruling, determination, claim or controversy, or other particular matter pertaining to any program requirement or a contract or sub-contract or any solicitation or proposal therefore pending before the school district.

It is a breach of ethics for any payment, gratuity or offer of employment to be made by or on behalf of a vendor/subcontractor under a contract to the prime vendor/contractor or higher tier sub-contractor for any contract with the school district, or any person associated therewith, as an inducement for the award of a sub-contract or order.

It is a breach of ethics for an employee to use the purchasing power of the school district to make private purchases, except where an "employee discount" program is provided. Employees should not have private purchases sent to the school district to be paid for by the employee. Such purchases may give school district patrons or other employees an erroneous impression that something dishonest is being perpetrated; may confuse vendors who believe they are conducting business with the school district, and may evade personal sales tax obligations, a violation of state sales tax statutes.

A Core Tenet

One of the fundamental principles underlying ethics in school administration is that every person in all dealings with the school system should be treated fairly and equally. Many of the statutory provisions and regulations are directed toward this objective. Fairness is an indispensable component in school business practices.

In the emerging area of electronic purchasing and other e-Business activities, because of the informality that sometimes occurs in the casualness of electronic communications, school leaders must give special attention to monitoring the financial affairs that are conducted electronically and take steps to insure that business thus conducted is in full compliance with both the "letter" and the "intent" of statutes and regulations.

Failure to do so can prove costly and embarrassing.

Chapter Fourteen

Financing School Construction—

School administrators are, for the most part, experiencing an era of expanding programs due to steadily increasing public demands and, with some exceptions, still burgeoning student populations. Either of these factors over a period of time can produce problems in meeting the demands for space—the need to build new facilities or remodel and expand existing school buildings.

The building and remodeling process is loaded with built-in problems. Small mistakes in the planning and contract stages can result in large problems in construction and subsequent phases. Legal pitfalls can result in a variety of future problems ranging from unsatisfactory buildings to lawsuits, liens or even more complex issues.

Successful building projects bring about great pride within the school district and throughout the entire community. In seeking that successful conclusion, school administrators must give careful attention to statutory requirements governing all phases of long-range planning, design, bidding, contracts and financing the construction.

State Department of Education Guidelines

Two methods for financing school construction can be found in Oklahoma Statutes.

School districts may use the Building Fund budget, currently authorized up to a maximum five (5) mills of the district's net assessed valuation, to construct facilities and for other designated uses. The second method is for voters to approve and the district issue general obligation bonds for specific purposes, with the bonds to be retired through ad valorem Sinking Fund taxes to be collected for a designated number of years.

Building Fund Method

Assuming the voters have made the building fund millage permanent, the district should receive the five (5) mills every year.

The only revenue going into the building fund is the five (5) mills of property taxes and interest earnings on the building fund, and possibly interest from bond funds if the school board has authorized that action. Because interest rates have been at historical lows for many years, most building funds are now operating almost solely on the five (5) mills of property taxes and any reserves from when interest rates were much higher.

Although the building fund process once was frequently used for construction of new facilities, few districts receive enough money through the building fund levy to actually construct a major school structure. Because of economic conditions, most districts have been forced to use the building funds for either utilities or for maintenance and custodial services salaries—leaving little or nothing available for construction.

A few districts that have sufficient building funds available also use those funds for security services, technology, and some minor building maintenance.

Bond Issue Method

General obligation bond issues traditionally have been the source of funding most school construction.

An *Administrator's Guide to School Construction Projects*, published by the Oklahoma State Department of Education, June 2010, with revisions February 2011, summarizes the authorized manner of obtaining funds for construction and other capital projects. That guide points out, "The indebtedness of a school district cannot exceed 10 percent, including existing indebtedness, of the assessed valuation of taxable property within the school district."

That publication specifically outlines the legal process for calling an election, setting election date, legal publication requirements for advertising the election, conduct of the election, setting date for the sale of approved bonds, advertising the sale of bonds, the bid process, and the preparation of transcript of the bond activity to seek approval by the Office of the Attorney General of Oklahoma.

The Constitution for the State of Oklahoma contains a similar provision.

There are restrictions on how money generated through the general obligation bonds may be used. The Guide, based on provisions of the Oklahoma Constitution and Oklahoma

State Statutes, explains that the school district may issue general obligation bonds for these purposes:

- Purchase of land
- Construction of new buildings
- Additions to existing buildings
- Renovation of existing buildings
- Purchase of school furniture and fixtures, and
- Purchase of school buses.

During recent years, the Oklahoma Legislature has given some leniency concerning buying equipment with bond proceeds. The law defining what bond "equipment" is has been modified over the years to include technology, subscriptions, school owned uniforms and textbooks.

Use of bond funds for purchases that are not clearly capital equipment items is questioned by many financial purists who prefer capital funds to be used for equipment with long-term life span. School district operational budgets often are not sufficient to cover costs of all new and replacement of equipment, and the use of bond issue proceeds for those purchases has become more common.

The equipment bond issues, though, cannot exceed five years duration. Bond proceeds to construct new buildings, remodel facilities, purchase land for future school use, and other similar projects can be issued for periods longer than five years.

Bond issues requested for use in purchasing transportation buses and related equipment must be submitted as a separate proposal when submitted to voters. The transportation proposal can be considered during the same school election as a building bond issue, but listed as a separate question on the ballot.

School districts have presented general obligation bond issue proposals in two variations.

Short Term Bond Issues

A General Obligation Bond Issue for clearly defined specific projects, with the debt to be retired in a short time period, usually less than 10 years, is a process that seems to most closely follow the intent of the law.

A school district can incur bond debt, with the total debt not to exceed 10 percent of the district's net assessed ad valorem property valuation. Thus, if a school district's total property valuation was $75,000,000.00, the district could, with voter approval, issue bonds up to $7,500,000.00. However, if the district had an outstanding debt of $2,500,000.00 from previous bond issues that had not yet been retired, a new bond issue would be limited to $5,000,000.00 since the existing obligation must be combined and cannot exceed the $7,500,000.00 amount set by the 10 percent limit.

The limit can change only if the district's net assessed valuation increases through new property going on the tax rolls or through revaluation of property by the County Assessor.

Deciding how quickly the debt is to be "paid off" by retiring the bonds is decided as part of the bond issue election process. School districts that are experiencing rapid growth, and in need of building new facilities quickly, often will choose to issue bonds for three to five years. That plan permits recovery of the debt capacity more quickly, thus permitting voters to consider a new bond issue for more construction or other authorized purposes.

School leaders need to be certain that school district patrons, the voters, are aware of the "pros" and "cons" of short-term bond issues. The annual sinking fund millage rate, the tax dollars collected to retire the bonds, is determined by calculating the amount of principal and interest payments needed for that year's payments. A short-term bond issue will require a higher sinking fund tax rate than if the debt were to be retired over a longer period. The short-term bond issues pay off more quickly, recovering the bonding capacity and permitting new bonds to be considered earlier.

School districts that are experiencing very rapid increases in student enrollment, and constantly needing to build facilities, often establish a plan of annually voting short-term bond issues, resulting in a program of retiring a bond issue annually and voting a new bond issue annually. That plan normally results in maintaining a stable tax rate while still adding the new bond issue each year.

Regardless of the debt retirement schedule, all of the outstanding bonds combined cannot exceed the 10 percent net assessed valuation of the district.

Multiple Year Series Bond Issues

Some school districts, usually larger districts, select a variation of the traditional General Obligation Bonds program by seeking voter authorization to issue a large amount of capital bonds using a series of multi-year bond sales. The bond sales are timed to insure that the district remains within the legal limits of the 10 percent debt capacity.

Voters could be asked to authorize future bond sales during specified multi-year periods to finance facilities, purchase of equipment, school buses and other needs authorized by law as part of a long-range plan. The requested authorization would exceed the district's immediate debt limit, but bonds would be issued in amounts and at intervals that insured the debt during the fiscal year did not exceed the legal 10 percent net assessed valuation limit.

Rather than voters being invited to approve an annual bond issue proposal, the school patrons are asked to give authority for bonds to be issued in the future, with the multi-year plan considered in one election. The bonds still must be issued and sold in the traditional manner, but in a series of sales over a specified period of years in order to comply with the 10 percent net assessed valuation limit.

The school district would have one election rather than a series of elections.

Whether school district patrons have clarity about location, time for construction and other details of specific projects could be questioned. That, in part, would depend on the publication of the long-range plans for the district. New residents who arrive during the years after such a proposal was approved by voters most likely would be unfamiliar with what was authorized in the years before they arrived in the community.

School administrators have an obligation to keep new residents properly informed about those plans and the district's debt-retirement obligations that were given voter approval in previous years.

Many school leaders are following those guidelines, closely observing the Constitutional and statutory requirements.

Creative Techniques

Creative financing techniques have been and are being used by many Oklahoma school districts that involve the creation of a public trust authority, or assistance of an existing public trust authority, through which revenue bonds are issued to obtain larger amounts of money for school construction than could be provided through the building bond process authorized for schools in the Oklahoma Constitution. The plan involves lease payments by the school district to the trust authority as the source of revenue to retire the bonds.

Many questions have been raised in recent years about lease agreements and the long-term financing commitments through the use of a public trust issuing revenue bonds. The "jury is still out" on this issue. In truth, at the time of writing of this book, no judge or jury are even reviewing any legal challenge of the "conduit financing" concept in Oklahoma. Various attorneys have offered legal advice, both pro and con, to school district leaders concerning the uses of the *Educational Facilities Lease Revenue Bonds* concept. Scores of school districts have used the concept to erect millions of dollars of new school facilities across the State—with the debt to be retired at some distant time in the future.

There are those who question whether the finance plan "squares" with the Oklahoma Constitution that provides for school district capital funds to be generated through a Building

Bond issue process. Others feel the plan is an innovative construction financing method that gives school districts an opportunity to have significant resources immediately to build new facilities years in advance of achieving an increase in the ad valorem tax base and the resulting bonding capacity for those facilities.

The school construction financing is not the schools' activity but is that of the "trust authority" that has contracted with the school district. The school district recommends to the trust authority what construction is desired. In most cases, the school district must lease the school land to the trust authority so the construction can take place on the school land, with the completed project sub-leased back to the school district. The trust authority proceeds with the desired construction project. The school district leases the buildings from the trust authority and makes annual lease payments to the trust to provide the revenue to retire the bonds, with those payments made from voter-approved general obligation bonds designed to generate the needed annual amount for lease payments.

Promotional Information

An examination of publications issued by school districts in the promotion of the bond issues through the conduit financing plan finds evidence that many districts are using the "bond money" to purchase a wide range of expendable items. One district's publicity explained, "The bond election calls for an allocation of $12 million for instructional supplies, including textbooks, equipment and materials." There wasn't an explanation of what the term, "materials," might include.

In one community where the lease-to-purchase bond issue plan was utilized, the newspaper coverage of the approaching election provided some explanation of the funding implications. The newspaper report explained that through a lease- purchase agreement with a community Educational Authority, "the school district will be able to take advantage of current construction costs and interest rates—benefits the district could not have taken immediate advantage of with existing debt caps." The newspaper article explained that the Educational Authority consisted of City Council members and "was formed to oversee the lease purchase." The article further explained that the Educational Authority would "take proceeds of the bank loan and construct the school facilities, leasing them to the school district until the loan is paid off."

One must assume that the City Council members who made up the newly created Education Authority would build the facilities that were requested by the Board of Education.

A spokesman for the school district was quoted as saying, "the lease payments made to the city will be $613,770.00 a year." Nothing was said about the number of years those payments would be made. The spokesman explained that the lease payments would be the school district's interest payment . . . and the interest cost would come out of the school district's Building Fund.

Thoughtful Questions

Some questions come to mind about this plan for financing school construction.

Dr. Kenneth Hancock, Professor and Assistant Dean of a university College of Education, is one of Oklahoma's recognized scholars in the field of Oklahoma School Finance Law and Practices. Scores of educators who desire to become school administrators—or prepare for advancement in the profession—have learned sound principles of *School Finance* and *School Law* in his classroom.

In responding to a request for his observations about methods currently being used for financing school construction, he pointed out that the *Educational Facilities Lease Revenue Bonds* concept had not been through a court review process, leaving a few basic questions unanswered.

He cited an example: "In this type of issue, if the district is basically in a lease-purchase type agreement with some trust authority, what happens if the school district decides to call off the lease-purchase agreement as a school district can in all other lease-purchases?"

He continued, "Does this type plan take away the ability of the district to stop a lease-purchase?"

Dr. Hancock theorized that if a district did not have a right to end the agreement, then the *Lease Revenue Bond* plan "would seem to be placing a district in debt outside the scope of what is allowed by the Oklahoma Constitution."

Among other questions he posed are the following:

- Can one vote be given for multiple bond questions?
- Can a bond election be held years before the bond issue takes place?
- Is a serial bond voted by a school district a school bond or a bond of the "trust authority" through which the bonds are being issued?

- Can a school district breach the Constitutional 10% debt limit rule by doing a serial bond?
- If a school district defaults on a serial bond, who is held responsible for payment of the debt?

School district leaders, superintendents in particular, have ethical and legal obligations to be certain that members of boards of education are well informed on the myriad of school-related issues that come before them as elected representatives of the public. There is some doubt that the majority of school board members have in-depth knowledge about the concept of *Educational Facilities Lease Revenue Bonds* method of financing school construction.

Following are some questions that need to be considered:

- Do the superintendents buying into this method of financing actually make certain their boards of education understand how this concept really works?
- If board members are in office to look after the public's interest and to be good stewards of the people's tax money, should not there be an obligation of the Board to inform the public of all aspects of a bond issue?
- If legal action against a school district for participating in this type of bond issue should become a reality, do the board members understand the consequences that may transpire?
- Since school board members have taken an oath to uphold the State Constitution, just as has the superintendent, does the superintendent have an

ethical obligation to advise the board members and the public about any pitfalls of such funding?

- Do those leading the bond campaign promotion have an obligation to inform the public of how this type plan works, as well as the "good" and the "bad" of the funding concept?

The legality of the lease revenue bond concept may be determined at some point in the future through some court review. The questions one must ask, though, are these:

- Does the average citizen know what is taking place?
- Does the school board really understand the plan?
- Does the school administrator comprehend the implications?

School administrators have an Ethical obligation to carefully explain the financing plan to patrons in the school district before they are asked to vote on a "School Bond" proposal using that concept.

Media information packets, school websites, brochures and other promotional information related to such school construction programs should adequately explain the *Educational Facilities Lease Revenue Bonds* financing plan.

That explanation should include the amount or percentage of the money that will be required for fees to the various parties involved in the financing plan, the interest rate for financing the project and the total amount of interest payments for the number of years required to retire the lease obligation.

CHAPTER FIFTEEN

Commercialization—A New Danger

Many school districts have initiated "Partners in Education," "Adopt-a-School" and similar programs to team with businesses in what began as mutually beneficial cooperative activities. Through such programs, schools have profited by receiving support in the form of personnel, technology and materials.

Some partnerships, though, have moved to a different level and have opened the school doors to questionable commercial ventures to supplement their budgets.

Legislative bodies, policy makers and other groups that seek to direct or control education continue to press school district officials to improve student performance while at the same time force embracement of efforts that constrain funding and spending on the programs and services that are needed to produce those mandated results. Tax reductions and expenditure limits have been imposed. Although tax and expenditure limits can provide business and individual citizens some tax relief, little is done to compensate schools for lost revenues.

School leaders have searched for alternative sources of revenue; and, in the process, an increasing number of school districts are using commercial activities to supplement their budgets—a controversial resource stream.[36]

Dr. Brian O. Brent, a Professor and Associate Dean at an university in New York state; and Stephen Lunden, an Assistant Superintendent of Schools in a New York state school district, reviewed how school districts across the nation have become involved in several types of commercial-type activities in an interesting article, "Pennies for Perils?," they wrote for the Association of School Business Officials International's *School Business Affairs* magazine.[37]

Their study and analysis reviews just how widespread school-based commercial activities has become. Most accounts of commercial activities can be found in the popular media, describing what might represent extraordinary activities, such as rights contracts and signage on top of school buildings near airports.

Following are some of the types of school-business relationships that have emerged:

Exclusive agreements: Districts grant businesses the exclusive right to sell or promote their products or services. Examples include pouring rights agreements and vending contracts.

Sponsorship of programs and activities: Businesses associate their name with a district event in exchange for paying for or subsidizing the event. Examples include

[36] Molnar, A., F. Boninger, and K. M. Libby. 2014. Schoolhouse commercialism leaves policymakers behind. National Education Policy Center, Boulder, CO, March.
[37] Brent, Brian O. and Lunden, Stephen. "Pennies for Perils? An Accounting of School-Based Commercial Activities, *School Business Affairs*, Association of School Business Officials (ASBO) International, Reston, Virginia. http://asbointl.org/publications-news/school-business-affairs/sba-article.

advertising with banners and handouts during an athletic contest or a play.

Appropriation of space: Districts allocate school space to businesses that then display their logo or advertisements. Examples include the allocation of space on scoreboards, rooftops, buses, textbook covers, and computer screens.

Incentive programs: Businesses give districts fiscal or in-kind resources (e.g., pizza) when school community members perform a given task. Examples include students and staff collecting vendor-specific product labels or receipts.

Sponsored educational materials: Businesses give the district instructional materials that highlight the business, while promising to serve a legitimate learning outcome. Mr. Peanut's Guide to Nutrition is one such example.

Electronic marketing: Businesses give districts technology to provide instructional programming in exchange for the right to advertise to students during the programs. Channel One is a prominent example of this type of activity.

Fund-raising: Businesses provide districts with products, which are then sold and distributed by students, with the profits shared between the district and the vendor. Candy and catalog sales are among the most visible examples of such activities.[38]

As a trade-off for construction funds, equipment and extra money for various purposes, some school districts in Oklahoma and elsewhere in the nation are signing up for lucrative contracts that grant multi-year, exclusive rights to soft drink companies and other firms to place advertising

---

[38] Ibid. Brent and Lundan

before students in classrooms, hallways, in athletic facilities and to market and distribute various products to captive customers—young people in schools.

Because of the financial challenges that many school systems are facing and the buying power of students and their parents, corporations are finding schools to be enticing places to do business; and, the executives of such companies are willing to spend large sums of money in order to promote and sell products.

Commercialism in schools is a trend that is reflected in the way products and advertising are being presented to student bodies and others. Some of the commercial effort is the result of business partnerships that have evolved from initial efforts of companies to provide limited supplies and services to schools and have led to serious marketing activity which some perceive as "disturbing" and "threatening."

There is a growing concern among various groups about the increase in commercial activity in schools. Superintendents of schools and other administrators whose better judgment may have been influenced by the vision of substantial new sources of revenue for the school budgets should be cautious about the activity.

Those who support commercial activities argue that they allow districts to secure much-needed non-tax revenues. Other proponents suggest that the activities foster students' understanding of the business sector and economy.

Despite those suggested benefits, others oppose school commercialism for a variety of reasons, including the following thoughts:

Commercial activities are unethical in that students are a "captive audience" with little, if any, ability to turn away from commercial messages; and that commercially supported online learning environments often gather marketing information about students, thereby violating their privacy rights.

Commercial activities often promote unhealthy products. Some opponents note that many products marketed or made available in schools have been linked to childhood obesity (e.g., sugary beverages, salty snacks, and fast food). Some also point to the mixed messages that children receive when they are taught about nutrition in health class, only to find "junk food" in the lunchroom vending machines.

Commercial activities corrupt instruction. Some argue that sponsored educational materials and electronic marketing usurp valuable instructional time and, in some instances, degrade instruction by providing biased information concerning health, social, and environmental issues.

Commercial activities promote consumerism. Some opponents fear that commercial activities promote consumerism, whereby students are encouraged to substitute market values for democratic values, undermining public schooling's civic function.[39]

One ethical issue is related to the debate about whether public school facilities should be commercial-free sites. School facilities are essentially owned by the public—the citizens who approved the bond issues or other funding used to construct the buildings. Thus, the question: Do school leaders have the

---

[39] Ibid. Brent and Lundan

right to "commercialize" those facilities with advertising or other contracts for other business use of the facilities?

In examining the legal and ethical issues, administrators should consider that the mixing of commercial interests with public education raises fundamental issues of public policy, curriculum content, proper relationship of educators to the students entrusted to them, and the values that the school embodies.

Additional money to support school functions is important. The health, privacy and rights of students and citizens are also important factors.

The debate on this issue is ongoing.

CHAPTER SIXTEEN

Test Your Ethics Quotient

An excellent way to conduct self-examination on personal "ethics" is to spend some time as an individual, or perhaps with two or three other close friends who also are administrators, and talk about how one has performed, or is likely to perform, when faced with a specific critical decision.

School administrators generally embrace the concepts expressed in the *AASA's Statement of Ethics for Educational Leaders*, those beliefs and behavioral standards adopted by the American Association of School Administrators. That *Statement*, in reality functions as a "Code" for administrators. The document is summarized in Appendix B of this book.

Such a soul-searching session of talking about some real-life scenarios of issues faced by superintendents of schools and other school leaders matches to some degree the process that was used in two research studies on superintendent ethics by Roy Dexheimer in 1968 and William Fenstermaker in 1994.

A summary of that research is found in Chapter 17 and in Appendix E.

Let's consider a few realistic scenarios that pose ethical dilemmas for school district administrators. Whether sitting alone or with some friends, take some quiet time to consider each scenario.

Choose one of the responses listed following each scenario as the decision you personally would most likely make if faced with that issue. After considering each scenario, and making a personal choice on the "what to do," compare your responses with the "recommended responses" that are listed and explained at the end of this activity.

Scenarios are similar to those included in the Dexheimer and Fenstermaker studies, with preferred decisions based on standards outlined in the *AASA Code of Ethics*, and reflecting opinions of experienced administrators.

Scenario 1—

You are attending, at school district expense, a major national conference of school administrators (such as the AASA convention). While there, you meet a group of friends in the hotel lobby. After a few moments your group is approached by the sales representative of a product used by all of your schools. He mingles with the group and before long insists that all of you accompany him to dinner at one of the city's better restaurants at his company's expense.

How do you respond to the invitation?

A. Accept with thanks.

B. Try to get the salesman aside, indicating that you would enjoy having dinner with him privately sometime.

C. Decline the invitation, claiming you have another commitment, even though this is not really the case.

D. Accept the invitation, but only if you are allowed to pay for your own meal.

E. None of the above, but rather . . .

Scenario 2—

Your school district is a rural one and quite homogeneous in its population. The teaching staff reflects this homogeneity— that is, they are mostly white, middle-class, and Protestant. In your search for new staff members, an excellent candidate with extremely promising credentials appears. The interview turns up the additional fact that this candidate belongs to a racial or ethnic group not generally found in your area (imagine any you wish). The board has made it clear in the past that all hiring is entirely in your hands; they'll ratify any recommendation you make to them.

How will you proceed?

A. You turn to other candidates, not out of prejudice, but as a form of protection for this applicant, who would clearly be in a lonely and vulnerable position if hired.

B. Hire the minority candidate on your own authority or allow the board to hear the facts and decide for itself.

C. Although other candidates are clearly inferior, you hire one of them as the best course of action for this particular community at this particular time.

D. You do not hire the candidate yourself, but you do make efforts to seek placement for him in the form of contacts you have in other districts.

E. None of the above, but rather . . .

Scenario 3—

The parents of a good student and generally responsible youngster have come to you with complaints about the teaching style of a social studies teacher. They claim he is using biased materials and slanted opinions in his classes. Further, they claim that when their son tried to question these approaches, he was greeted with sarcasm and thinly veiled threats to have his grades lowered. The father is well known for his involvement in civic and community affairs, and he demands evidence of your immediate action.

What is your response?

A. Agree with the parents that the teacher is in the wrong, and indicate that censure will be applied in some form.

B. Have the boy transferred to another classroom with a teacher whose techniques and methods are well known to you and which you know will placate these irate parents.

C. Call the most immediate supervisor of the teacher and ask for some corroboration of the incidents; then proceed with action.

D. Indicate to the parents that you will take the matter up with the teacher and his supervisors, but that no direct action will be taken until both sides of the controversy have been aired.

E. None of the above, but rather . . .

Scenario 4—

A local service organization, of which you are a member, puts on an impressive talent show annually to raise funds. This year they have designated the proceeds to help the AFS

Exchange Student Program in your school. All rehearsals and the final show will be in the high school auditorium. The chair of the talent show has come to you to ask for a reduction in the normal rates charged by the school for the use of the facilities, so that a maximum profit may be realized.

As superintendent, and a member of the organization, how do you respond?

A. You recommend to the board that the request be granted.

B. Refuse the request, point out the policy as it stands, and note that other equally deserving groups use the auditorium during the year.

C. Since the request will mean more benefits to the district's AFS program, you grant it as an administrative action.

D. You give no definite answer, but urge the chair to state his or her case before the board, with your support guaranteed.

E. None of the above, but rather . . .

Scenario 5—

You and others see that your supervisor is showing favoritism to an employee. The favored employee is allowed to adjust his time schedule to accommodate some personal needs. Other employees in the department have asked to adjust their time schedules, but are not given this opportunity.

What should you do?

A. Talk to your supervisor about the situation.

B. Ignore the situation. That's just the way some supervisors are and nothing can be done to change the situation.

C. Take the issue to higher level (to the assistant superintendent or superintendent of schools).

D. None of the above, but rather . . .

Scenario 6—

You, as a night plant operations department supervisor, suspect that a co-worker has been drinking alcohol on the job.

What should you do?

A. Notify your immediate supervisor/administrator of your suspicions.

B. Approach the co-worker and discuss the situation.

C. Ignore the situation. It's a personal issue.

D. None of the above, but rather . . .

Scenario 7—

You recently were promoted to a senior administrative position in the school system and received a Corporate American Express Card. Since employees are responsible for paying his/her bills, you used the corporate credit card to pay for a recent meal for your wife and some friends when the group dined at a nice restaurant. Can you use the school card for such "personal expenses"?

Possible answers:

A. Not sure. Ask another administrator.

B. Contact the American Express office

C. Yes. Since an employee is personally responsible for paying the bill each month, it should be allowable to charge personal expenses.

D. No. It is against school district policy.

E. None of the above, but rather . . .

Scenario 8—

You are an assistant principal. While in the school district administrative center, you witness a supervisor sign the name of an assistant superintendent on an important document that must be submitted to the Board of Education for review and action. The administrator tells you he has authority to sign for the assistant superintendent, but you have reason to doubt that administrator's word.

What action should you take?

A. Do nothing, because you know that central office administrator can make your life miserable if you challenge him.

B. Suggest that the supervisor telephone the assistant superintendent and inform him/her that he is signing his/her name to the document.

C. Make the assistant superintendent or superintendent aware of the situation.

D. None of the above, but rather . . .

Scenario 9—

On a recent business trip you stayed at a hotel that provided a free breakfast. You accepted the free breakfast each morning of your stay. You believe it is okay to submit an expense reimbursement for a set amount for breakfast each morning since it is your understanding that the school district allows you a certain dollar amount for breakfast.

Is that okay?

Possible answers:

A. No. An employee should be sure that the reimbursement claim is accurate and complete.

B. Yes. You are aware that others in the school system have done the same thing.

C. None of the above, but rather . . .

Scenario 10—

You decide to rent a car for an out-of-town school business trip instead of driving your own car and requesting reimbursement for mileage and related expenses. While preparing your reimbursement claim, you determine that you could receive extra money if you claimed the mileage for your personal car instead of the costs related to the rental car.

What should you do?

A. Claim the mileage reimbursement. You deserve a little extra for traveling out of town.

B. File the claim for the cost of the rental car only.

C. None of the above, but rather . . .

The Answers—

Based on review by several experienced administrators, applying individual interpretations of the *AASA Code of Ethics* and arriving at consensus opinions, the following responses are considered the most appropriate action for each scenario:

Scenario 1.

D. Accept the invitation, but only if you are allowed to pay for your own meal.

Rationale: Avoiding a situation that might leave one with a feeling of an "obligation" to a company or sales representative is important for future business transactions. The reason could be quietly explained to the sales representative in a one-to-one discussion.

Scenario 2.

B. Hire the minority candidate on your own authority or allow the board to hear the facts and decide for itself.

Rationale: The best-qualified candidate available should be employed. The applicant probably should be made aware of the community demographics as he/she considers accepting an offered contract.

Scenario 3.

D. Indicate to the parents that you will take the matter up with the teacher and his supervisors, but that no direct action will be taken until both sides of the controversy have been aired.

Rationale: Fairness, loyalty and respect for all people are basic convictions of a good leader. Careful "listening" to all parties and a study of both sides of an issue are critical steps in reaching a wise decision.

Scenario 4.

B. Refuse the request, point out the policy as it stands, and note that other equally deserving groups use the auditorium during the year.

Rationale: School district policies should be applied in a consistent manner, even when there is a personal preference to grant an exception. Granting a policy waiver for one organization would prompt others to seek similar privilege.

Scenario 5.

C. Take the issue to higher level.

Rationale: Since the supervisor is allowing only one employee the opportunity to adjust his time schedule, it would be best to make a higher-level administrator of the issue.

Scenario 6.

A. Notify your immediate supervisor/administrator of your suspicions.

Rationale: Reporting this situation to senior management as soon as possible is important, not only for concerns about safety of students and staff, but also to avoid personal injury to the individual or damage to school property. Approaching the co-worker on a personal level may be an option and would give him or her the opportunity to take care of the problem through some employee assistance program.

Scenario 7.

D. No. It is against school district policy (or should be against policy).

Rationale: Personal use of a school district credit card is inappropriate, and may lead to cancellation of the card as well as disciplinary action. Normally, such cards may be used to cover such expenses as airfare, lodging, rental cars, meals while at conference, other business-related travel expenses. A corporate card is provided as a tool to more efficiently cover business-related expenses.

A best practice is to use personal credit cards, pay the expenses, and seek reimbursement for appropriate official school business expenses on an itemized expense report form.

Scenario 8.

B. Suggest that the supervisor telephone the assistant superintendent and inform him/her that he is signing his/her name to the document;

Or,

C. Make the assistant superintendent or superintendent aware of the situation.

Rationale: If you believe the actions are improper, you should speak up and address the matter.

Scenario 9.

A. No. An employee should be sure that the reimbursement claim is accurate and complete.

Rationale: Employees should only submit a reimbursement request for expenses they actually incur. If an employee accepts the free breakfast offered at a hotel, the employee should not submit a charge for that breakfast. If the employee ate breakfast elsewhere and paid, then it is an appropriate expense.

Scenario 10.

B. File the claim for the cost of the rental car only.

Rationale: Employees should only submit claims for expenses they actually incur.

CHAPTER SEVENTEEN

Superintendents—Past and Present

Superintendents who are occupying the school CEO offices across the land regularly make decisions that involve ethical choices. How do the superintendents of the new era, the 2000's, compare with the superintendents of a more than a quarter-century ago when it comes to making ethical choices?

That question was the focus of a doctoral study by William C. Fensternmaker, a Pennsylvania administrator, who conducted a study of members of the American Association of School Administrators in "The Ethical Dimension of Superintendent Decision Making: A Study of AASA Members."

This project was an update of a similar study conducted in 1968 by long-time AASA member C. Roy Dexheimer, a superintendent in New York state. Dexheimer found that superintendents frequently made choices that were inconsistent with the *AASA Code of Ethics.* One would hope that modern-day administrators would make decisions, which more closely adhere to the ethical guidelines of the profession. Sadly, for the state of the administrative profession, Fensternmaker's findings, with few exceptions, nearly duplicated the findings in the 1968 study.

In the two studies, superintendents were asked to respond to a borderline ethical dilemma—typically a minor problem of a routine nature—designed to elicit a response or choice of action. The dilemmas approximated situations that most administrators likely would encounter at some time. Of the choices provided, only one would have been considered appropriate based on the guidelines and examples of the *AASA Code of Ethics.*

A panel of AASA Executive Committee members completed the survey, indicating the choices that they considered "most ethical," to serve as another guide for scoring responses. The majority replies from this panel produced a second standard against which the superintendent responses were compared.

The study found that there was very little change in the ethical responses of the 1968 superintendents and those in office in 1996.

Dexheimer recorded 1,725 ethical responses on the dilemma scenarios out of a possible total of 3,630, or 47.3 percent. Using the same criteria, Fensternmaker's study recorded 1,341 ethical replies out of a possible 2,790, or 48.1 percent. The majority of responses to both surveys were unethical, with the difference less than one percentage point from then to now, suggesting no significant change over time.

Both studies found variations relative to enrollment, with a tendency for scores to be higher (or more ethical) for superintendents in larger school systems. Scores were as much as 10 points higher among superintendents in districts with more than 20,000 students.

Also, both studies found variations relative to salary, with a tendency for scores to be higher among superintendents receiving the highest salaries. With the exception of a small group at the lowest salary level, scores showed a steady increase as salary increases, with the differences again as great as 10 points or more.

And, both studies found variations relative to experience. While not as pronounced as the salary and enrollment variations, the studies noted a tendency for higher scores among those superintendents with fewer years of service, both in their current district and overall.

One difference between the 1996 data and that from 1968 was noteworthy. Dexheimer, in 1968, found his subjects reporting the majority of their ethical replies as coming from actual experience. The 1996 study instead found the majority of non-ethical replies coming from actual experience. This may suggest that modern-day superintendents are even less ethical in actual practice than were their counterparts in 1968.

The results of the study strongly indicate that the matter of ethics in administrative decision-making has not received adequate attention. The survey responses from superintendents nationwide showed either a severe confusion about ethical standards or a disturbing disregard of them.

Either superintendents are unaware of the ethical factors suffused in the issues they face or they simply do not care. Whichever is the case, the matter clearly requires attention.

The study results should be cause for concern among all parts of the education community, but especially among superintendents.

Included among Fensternmaker's recommendations are such things as urging the administrators' professional organizations to reestablish an emphasis on ethical behavior as a high priority for members; to focus on "policing" the profession; for the profession to become more vocal about its position on ethical issues and more firm with its members to create a heightened sense of awareness and accountability; and for institutions of higher education which are involved in administrator training programs to implement coursework in the ethical factors that relate to school and district administration.

These are good recommendations.

Administrators, at all levels, cannot afford to become another "distrusted" profession in America. The continued success of superintendents and other school administrators depends on trust and credibility. It is absolutely necessary for superintendents to know and conscientiously apply ethical principles in their work roles. Otherwise, as Fensternmaker pointed out, "the alternative will be a gradual degradation of the profession as a whole—a loss of trust eventually extending not only to superintendents, but to the entire public school system that they represent.

Chapter Eighteen

Squeaky Clean on Critical Issues

"Skirting" issues or a harboring a desire to "slightly bend the rules" can be a temptation when dealing with some of the varied and often controversial topics, which are involved, in the administration and governance of a school district. A list comes to mind of topics which, even though sometimes unpleasant, need to be dealt with in a "squeaky-clean" manner. Those areas of concern include topics such as Nepotism, Employee Termination, Competitive Bidding, Travel and Conference Expenses, Open Meeting Law, Executive Sessions, Ethics in Bargaining, Open Records, Privileged Communications, Staff Employment.

This is not a complete list—only some examples. But, this list includes topics which can be controversial, topics on which the law and regulations are very precise, and topics where there are known instances of ignoring the rules, bending the rules, skirting issues and similar action which indicate that some administrators sometimes are challenged.

Let's examine in a cursory manner a few of the areas which need the "squeaky-clean" approach by school administrators— all the time, every time, no exceptions. That "squeaky-clean" approach makes it much easier for one to rest in the knowledge that the action taken was precisely how the law intended.

Nepotism

Favoritism shown or patronage granted to relatives, as in business, is the simplest way to describe this topic. A related matter is that of Conflict of Interest when an administrator has the potential for personal gain through some personal action, or through action, which the administrator leads others, including a Board of Education, to consider.

There are at least three major areas of Nepotism concern, which need to be understood. Those are: employment of relatives, contracts with relatives, and conflicts of interest.

Although the school administrator doesn't function under the same legal restrictions, which apply to a Board of Education, following the same guidelines may be wise when it comes to Nepotism and Conflict of Interest issues.

Employment of relatives is an area which can cause grief to administrators. Such action is prohibited for school board members. Administrators—superintendents of schools in particular—should follow the same guidelines in order to maintain a "squeaky-clean" appearance with the public.

The "degrees" of relationship are well defined in Oklahoma School Law. Those lists are easy to find. The law has been modified several times, often in an attempt to address a specific case. There are some "ifs, ands and buts" in the law. But, the real intent is well-known: There aren't supposed to be any close family relationships between Board Members and employees in the district; and, ethically, the superintendent should place himself or herself under similar restrictions.

The best advice is if there appears to be a conflict of interest, there probably is, in reality, a conflict. Don't do it! Avoid showing favoritism or patronage in any form to relatives. Avoid any situation which has the potential for personal gain or personal gain for a relative.

In summary, in thinking about Nepotism, remember these areas of concern, which should be avoided:

- Employment of relatives.
- Contracts with relatives.
- Conflicts of interest.

Travel and Conference Expenses

Although this topic can be far-reaching, let's concentrate on some danger areas when asking for the use of public funds to cover expenses incurred while an administrator is in some official status as a representative of the school district.

Based on school district policy and terms of contract, administrators may be extended authorization to incur expenses, within the limitations provided by law, as they conduct official business of the school district. Most school districts have very complete policies, which outline school finance procedures.

Just as is true in many business organizations, keeping close tab on expenses related to official travel is difficult. Some administrators are tempted to take advantage of the system and sometimes submit requests for reimbursement of costs, which, although they may have occurred while in a travel status as a representative of the school district, are simply personal costs. Let's examine one problem example:

Several members of a Board of Education, accompanied by the Superintendent, attended an out-of-state conference. After completing registration, the four persons rented a car, drove to a resort and nationally known golf course located more than 100 miles from the conference city, spent the entire day and evening at the resort location. The scenario was repeated a second day at a different golf course. The costs of the meals, which also included purchase of alcoholic beverages, the rental of the car, purchase of gasoline, and disguised "greens fees," were included in reimbursed conference expenses.

Were those legitimate expenses for the conference?

Serious issues—both ethical and legal—face the superintendent of schools in dealing with travel and conference reimbursement expenses in such a situation.

Among personal expenses which often show up in payment of travel and conference expenses are such things as purchase of athletic event tickets, movie rentals charged to hotel rooms, alcoholic beverages, meals for spouses, sometimes travel expenses for spouses, car rentals for personal side-trips, hotel expenses for extra days (before or after the conference) for vacation time for member and/or family. There are other examples, but you get the idea.

Necessary itemized and documented travel and conference expenses are very appropriate.

Apply the following newspaper test when filing your conference and travel expenses: "How would the list of expenses look if printed on Page One of the local newspaper?" If you are comfortable with the list after that question, then the expenses are probably all very legitimate.

There are hundreds of examples—many of which have been dealt with in Opinions by the Attorney General or through the courts—which illustrate that there are some people who simply do not want to follow the intent of the law in this area.

The best advice is: If there appears to be a conflict of interest, there probably is, in reality, a conflict. Don't do it!

When it comes to travel and conference expenses, remember:

- Don't be tempted to take advantage of the system
- Carefully avoid reimbursement of personal costs
- Necessary itemized expenses are very appropriate
- Apply the newspaper test when filing travel expenses

Open Meeting Law and Executive Sessions

Nothing can void the best-intended action of conducting school business faster than the carelessness of violating the strict provisions of the Oklahoma Open Meeting Act. The intent of that act is to guarantee that the "public's business" is conducted "in the public." That law is not intended to make a board meeting a "public forum," but simply to guarantee that the business discussion and action is handled out in the open within the viewing and hearing of the public.

That seems simple enough. Yet, there is a tendency to attempt to conduct the public's business and times and places which are not convenient to the public, to take action "behind closed doors," to meet and discuss business when not in an official meeting, and to leave the impression of being secretive about the public's business.

One important role of the superintendent of schools is to insist that this and other statutes are carefully honored.

It is the official public policy of the State of Oklahoma to encourage and facilitate an informed citizenry's understanding of the governmental processes and governmental problems. A school district is an official sub-division of state government. The official public policy is to do everything in a way, which improves the opportunity for the public to be informed and to understand "what's going on."

There are many examples of how that official policy is circumvented by intentional or careless acts of board members. Areas where problems are most likely to occur are conducting "hurry up" meetings which do not meet time and notice restrictions, handling business in informal gatherings or through telephone, facsimile, e-mail or other communications which avoid the required openness, and using the executive session time to discuss topics which are not appropriate for discussion in the closed session and which were not listed in the agenda listing advising of a planned executive session and which were not included in the motion used to authorize the board entering into such a session.

The superintendent of schools, with his or her knowledge of statutes and regulations, has an ethical obligation to be the moral compass for the board and others who may want to follow inappropriate procedures.

Sometimes, a member of the administration or the school board will "get an idea" during a meeting and want to place another item on the table for a vote. Unless the topic has been properly listed in the published agenda, with precise information that there will be discussion of and consideration of a vote on the matter, action should not be taken on a non-agenda topic. The superintendent's role is to provide the guidance.

The proper procedure is to table the matter and refer the topic for review, discussion and action at a future meeting. Taking a vote without properly meeting the requirements of notice and agenda listing is not appropriate. The action, if challenged, could be voided. During the heat of discussion, participants in the meeting do not want to hear that "we can't vote on that item." Nevertheless, a proposed vote should be blocked so that the meeting can be "squeaky-clean" in compliance with the Open Meeting Law.

The superintendent has the ethical obligation to insist that the law be observed.

Probably the chief offender in violation of the Open Meeting Law, though, is in the area of abusing the right for executive session.

Who knows if there has been a violation in an executive session? Obviously, everyone who participates in the session knows what is being done, and any one of those in attendance—but most certainly the superintendent of schools—is in a position to advise the others "this topic really isn't appropriate for discussion in this executive session so let's stop it."

The superintendent of schools knows that executive sessions of the board of education are permitted only for very specific reasons, carefully defined in the statutes. Generally, those sessions are held for discussing the employment, hiring, appointment, promotion, demotion, discipline or resignation of an employee; discussing negotiations concerning collective bargaining; discussing the purchase or appraisal of real property; reviewing confidential communications between the board and the attorney concerning some pending action, and some specific areas related to specific handicapped children.

Notice that the law only refers to "discussing." Taking a vote, taking an opinion poll, reaching agreement on a planned vote, etc., is inappropriate, and in some cases downright illegal.

Administrators and board members often want to go into executive session to discuss a salary increase for a specific employee, to talk about a complaint someone has made, or to discuss the won-loss record of the football coach. Those are not authorized reasons. Sometimes, persons in an executive session, which has been called for a very legitimate reason, may want to open up discussion on several other topics. That expanded discussion should be avoided. Again, the superintendent of schools has the ethical obligation to serve as the group's "moral compass."

When it comes to the Open Meeting Law, remember that the intent of the act is to guarantee that the "public's business" is conducted "in the public," but it is not a "public forum." The superintendent has an ethical obligation to avoid any tendency to do any of the following:

- To conduct the public's business at places and times not convenient to the public
- To take action "behind closed doors"
- To meet and discuss business when not in an official meeting

- To leave the impression of being secretive about the public's business.

Ethics in Bargaining

There has been only a little research in the important and often disputed aspect of the role of the superintendent of schools in the collective bargaining process. Since the superintendent serves as an exoffico member of the school board, and since that group retains the position of being the ultimate decision making authority for the school district in the area of employee relations, there is good argument that both the superintendent and board members should be careful to avoid direct involvement in the "at-table" process. The superintendent has a critical role in the strategy sessions, which may be held in executive session, but individual, personal involvement in either an official or unofficial manner can be dangerous, as well as unethical.

During the time when negotiations are continuing, the superintendent of schools and other administrators should refrain from talking about specific issues with the public on any matters related to negotiations and, certainly, should refrain from meeting with or talking with teachers or other persons involved in the collective bargaining unit about those items being negotiated.

When it comes to Ethics in Bargaining, the superintendent of schools must remember that the school board is the ultimate decision-making authority and the most appropriate role for the superintendent is in strategy sessions with the board of education and others. The superintendent and other administrators who are involved in the strategy session must remember the following:

- Keep executive session talk inside that room.
- Avoid private involvement in "side-bar" negotiations.

Bribery, Gratuities and Rewards

An administrator who yields to some overwhelming desire for gain and who offers, accepts or agrees to accept from another person or organization some monetary or other benefit of value as consideration for a decision, opinion, recommendation, vote or other exercise of discretion as a public servant has succumbed to bribery. That behavior is both unethical and illegal. It could rise to the level of a charge of felony.

The unethical behavior also extends to action by an administrator in seeking or accepting any benefit or compensation—after the fact—in recognition of an administrator having given a decision or for having otherwise exercised a discretion in favor of some individual, company or group, or accepting compensation for advice or other assistance in preparing or promoting a contract, claim, or other transaction or proposal when the administrator knows that he or she has or is likely to have some official involvement in developing a recommendation for action or in exercising some discretionary action..

Conflicts of Interest

Since the confidence of the citizenry is the very foundation for effective school government, even an unfounded appearance of unethical conduct by an administrator or other school employee can significantly impair the capability of the school system. Thus, avoiding even the appearance of a conflict of interest forms the basis for the good ethical behavior. The office of the Superintendent of Schools or any other school leader must not to be used for unauthorized personal gain. Any conflict between personal interests and official responsibility must be resolved by consciously avoiding possible conflicts or disclosing the basis of a possible conflict to so that, if necessary, decisions can be reviewed or made by others who can be totally objective.

A conflict of interest is a situation in which an individual— whether superintendent, administrator, employee or some other professional—has a private or personal interest sufficient to appear to influence the objective exercise of his or her official duties. There are three key elements to be considered:

First, there is a private or personal interest. Often this is a financial interest, but it could also be another sort of interest, say, to provide a special advantage to a spouse or child.

Second, the problem comes when this private interest comes into conflict with the definition, an "official duty" — quite literally the duty the administrator has acting in some official capacity. As a professional, especially one in a public school setting, the administrator takes on certain official responsibilities which include obligations to citizens, the school board, school employees, or others. These obligations are supposed to trump all private or personal interests.

Third, conflicts of interest interfere with professional responsibilities in a specific way, namely, by interfering with objective professional judgment. A major reason professionals are valued is that the citizens of a community, and certainly the school board members and school staff, expect the school district leaders to be objective and independent. Factors, like private and personal interests, that either interfere or appear likely to interfere with objectivity become a legitimate concern to those who have placed trust in the superintendent of schools or another administrator.

It is important to avoid apparent and potential as well as actual conflicts of interests. An apparent conflict of interest is one which a reasonable person would think that the administrator's judgment is likely to be compromised. A potential conflict of interest involves a situation that may develop into an actual conflict of interest.

In attempting to determine whether a situation is likely to interfere or appear to interfere with an administrator's independent judgment, one should apply the "trust test." Ask the following: "Would relevant others (school board, students, teachers, professional colleagues, or the general public) trust my judgment if they knew I was in this situation?"

Trust is at the ethical heart or core of this issue. Conflicts of interest involve the abuse, actual or potential, of the trust people have in a superintendent of schools or other school professionals. This is why conflicts of interest not only injure particular business and professional relationships, but they also damage the whole profession by reducing the trust people generally have in school administrators.

A second way to avoid conflicts of interests is for the administrator to absent himself or herself from decision-making or advice giving if there is a perception that the administrator may have a private interest in the action being considered. This probably is the wisest course of action.

Some skill and good judgment are required in order to recognize that one is in a conflict of interest situation. This is because private and personal interests can cloud a person's objectivity. It is easier to recognize when others are in a conflict, than when a personal problem exists. Thus, when in doubt, a wise approach is to talk with a trusted colleague or friend to get an unbiased opinion. But, find a friend who will be honest in the evaluation and recommendation.

Avoiding conflicts of interest is only one part of being a conscientious professional. Another part is the difficult task of making choices when the ethics of the situation aren't clear. A wise and ethical administrator must avoid such conflicts, especially in all school business matters, such as procurement practices and contract management.

In the preparation of any contract, bid or other similar agreement, a school administrator must carefully consider if there is any possible conflict of interest, or even the perception of such a conflict, which is associated with the agreement. The administrator should be able to certify the following statements:

1. To the best of my knowledge, neither I nor my spouse, dependent child, general partner, or any organization for which I am serving as an officer, director, trustee, general partner or employee, or any person or organization with whom I am negotiating or have an arrangement concerning prospective employment has a financial interest in this matter.

2. To the best of my knowledge, this matter will not affect the financial interests of any member of my household. Also, to the best of my knowledge, no member of my household; no relative with whom I have a close relationship; no one with whom my spouse, parent or dependent child has or seeks employment; and no organization with which I am seeking a business relationship nor which I now serve actively or have served within the last year are parties or represent a party to the matter.

3. I acknowledge my responsibility to disclose the acquisition of any financial or personal interest as described above that would be affected by the matter, and to disclose any interest I, or anyone noted above, has in any person or organization that does become involved in, or is affected at a later date by, the conduct of this matter.

Knowing and following all the many and varied laws is difficult. Most administrators want to be good stewards of the public's funds and to represent the public in a very professional way. "Skirting" issues or "slightly bending the rules" when dealing with some of the many, varied, and often controversial topics, which are part of administering a school district, must be avoided at all costs.

Every administrator should be totally committed to being "Squeaky-Clean on Critical Issues."

CHAPTER NINETEEN

Thou Shalt and Shalt Not

The Biblical Ten Commandments which were engraved on stone tablets and given by God to Moses—the great leader, lawgiver, and prophet of the ancient Israelites—are the heart of the law in the Old Testament; and, to a large degree, form the basis of much modern law in America.

Man has seen fit to expand those concisely worded commandments with millions of pages of statutes and regulations.

Attempting to list every ethical issue that a school administrator might face isn't realistic. Many have been discussed—some in summary and some at length—in various sections of this book. But, there are many other issues that come to mind and which, at least, need to be mentioned if only in a list.

There are a number of statutes that establish standards to which an administrator's conduct must conform. The following list is not comprehensive, but does include references to statutes of general applicability.

Consider these "Thou shalt" and "Thou shalt not" standards:

Ten Commandments for School Administrators

1. The prohibition against accepting bribe, money, property, thing of value in nature of commission for purchase of supplies, furniture or bonds.

   (§70-6-110)

2. The prohibition against solicitation or receipt of illegal gratuities.

   (§70-16-123)

3. The prohibition against receiving inducements for requiring purchase of particular materials; or soliciting free review instructional materials.

   (§70-3241.2)

4. The prohibition against placing school district funds in a school or public foundation.

   (§70-5-145)

5. The prohibition against gratuities or rewards in connection with employment of teachers.

   (§70-6-112)

6. The mandate to report expenditures, cost descriptions, amounts of funds spent, types of transactions, copies of credit card statements, and current per pupil expenditure figures.

   (§70-135.4)

7. The prohibition against fraud or false statements in settlement of claims, transfer of property, or payments.

   (§62-372)

8. The prohibition against claiming out-of-state students in calculation of student membership for state financial aid.

   (§70-18-111)

9. The prohibition against permitting students to be truant; the requirement to report truancy of students to Department of Human Services when student has not met 80 percent attendance standard.

   (§70-24-120)

10. The prohibition against advocating certain unlawful acts, criminal syndicalism, sabotage, sedition or treason upon public school grounds, including printing, circulating, distributing, displaying printed material advocating, advising, affirmatively suggesting, or teaching crime, or the commission of crime.

    (§21-1327)

Appendix A

Glossary of Terms

Culture

Shared values by system members that produce norms shaping individual and group behavior.

Employee

A person employed by a prospective contractor and subject to the prospective contractor's supervision and control as to the time, place, and manner of performance, who neither exerts nor proposes to exert improper influence to solicit or obtain contracts.

Established Commercial Selling Agency

A business that neither exerts nor proposes to exert improper influence to solicit or obtain public contracts. In determining whether a business is a bona fide established commercial selling business, the following factors should be considered: Whether the business is presently a going concern and is likely to continue as such.

Ethics

The set of principles, rules or standards governing the conduct of a person or the members of a profession; the rightness or wrongness of certain actions, and to the goodness or badness of the motives and ends of such action.

Gratuity

A payment, loan, subscription, advance, deposit of money, services, or anything of more than nominal value, present or promised, unless consideration of substantially equal or greater value is received.

Integrity

Steadfast adherence to a strict moral or ethical code.

Moral

Conforming to established standards of good behavior, rules of conduct, especially of sexual conduct, of or concerned with the judgment or instruction of goodness or badness of character and behavior.

Official Responsibility

Direct administrative or operating authority, whether intermediate or final, either exercisable alone or with others, either personally or through subordinates, to approve, disapprove, or otherwise direct school/organization action.

Procurement

To obtain, acquire, bring about, effect by special effort.

Prima Facie

A Latin term for "at first glance." It signifies an initial status of an idea or principle. In ethics, it stands for a duty that has a presumption in its favor but may be overridden by another duty.

Principle

A basic truth, law or assumption, a rule or standard—especially of good behavior, moral or ethical standards or judgments, a fixed or predetermined policy.

Society

Human beings collectively, a group of persons with a common culture or way of life, a group of people united in a common interest.

Standard

A norm or requirement of moral conduct; the criterion established for making moral or ethical judgments.

Trust

A firm reliance on the integrity, ability, or character of a person or organization; the condition of having confidence placed in one.

Values

Ideals, customs, and beliefs of system members toward which a group has an affectionate regard.

Vendor

One that makes something, such as a service or product, available; a provider.

Virtuous

Moral excellence and righteousness, an example of a kind of moral excellence, effective force of power.

Appendix B

American Association of School Administrators (AASA)
Statement of Ethics for Educational Leaders (Revised Version: 2009)

An educational leader's professional conduct must conform to an ethical code of behavior, and the code must set high standards for all educational leaders. The educational leader provides professional leadership across the district and also across the community. This responsibility requires the leader to maintain standards of exemplary professional conduct while recognizing that his or her actions will be viewed and appraised by the community, professional associates and students.

The educational leader acknowledges that he or she serves the schools and community by providing equal educational opportunities to each and every child. The work of the leader must emphasize accountability and results, increased student achievement, and high expectations for each and every student.

To these ends, the educational leader subscribes to the following statements of standards.

The educational leader—

1. Makes the education and well being of students the fundamental value of all decision making.
2. Fulfills all professional duties with honesty and integrity and always acts in a trustworthy and responsible manner.
3. Supports the principle of due process and protects the civil and human rights of all individuals.
4. Implements local, state and national laws.
5. Advises the school board and implements the board's policies and administrative rules and regulations.
6. Pursues appropriate measures to correct those laws, policies, and regulations that are not consistent with sound educational goals or that are not in the best interest of children.
7. Avoids using his/her position for personal gain through political, social, religious, economic or other influences.
8. Accepts academic degrees or professional certification only from accredited institutions.
9. Maintains the standards and seeks to improve the effectiveness of the profession through research and continuing professional development.
10. Honors all contracts until fulfillment, release or dissolution mutually agreed upon by all parties.
11. Accepts responsibility and accountability for one's own actions and behaviors.

12. Commits to serving others above self.

(Reprinted with permission from *School Administrator* magazine, a publication of AASA, the School Superintendents Association.)

APPENDIX C

Society of Professional Journalists
Code of Ethics
Preamble

Members of the Society of Professional Journalists believe that public enlightenment is the forerunner of justice and the foundation of democracy. The duty of the journalist is to further those ends by seeking truth and providing a fair and comprehensive account of events and issues. Conscientious journalists from all media and specialties strive to serve the public with thoroughness and honesty. Professional integrity is the cornerstone of a journalist's credibility. Members of the Society share a dedication to ethical behavior and adopt this code to declare the Society's principles and standards of practice.

Seek Truth and Report It
Journalists should be honest, fair and courageous in gathering, reporting and interpreting information.

Journalists should:

Test the accuracy of information from all sources and exercise care to avoid inadvertent error. Deliberate distortion is never permissible.

- Diligently seek out subjects of news stories to give them the opportunity to respond to allegations of wrongdoing.
- Identify sources whenever feasible. The public is entitled to as much information as possible on sources' reliability.
- Always question sources' motives before promising anonymity. Clarify conditions attached to any promise made in exchange for information. Keep promises.
- Make certain that headlines, news teases and promotional material, photos, video, audio, graphics, sound bites and quotations do not misrepresent. They should not oversimplify or highlight incidents out of context.
- Never distort the content of news photos or video. Image enhancement for technical clarity is always permissible. Label montages and photo illustrations.
- Avoid misleading reenactments or staged news events. If reenactment is necessary to tell a story, label it.
- Avoid undercover or other surreptitious methods of gathering information except when traditional open methods will not yield information vital to the public. Use of such methods should be explained as part of the story.
- Never plagiarize.

- Tell the story of the diversity and magnitude of the human experience boldly, even when it is unpopular to do so.
- Examine their own cultural values and avoid imposing those values on others.
- Avoid stereotyping by race, gender, age, religion, ethnicity, geography, sexual orientation, disability, physical appearance or social status.
- Support the open exchange of views, even views they find repugnant.
- Give voice to the voiceless; official and unofficial sources of information can be equally valid.
- Distinguish between advocacy and news reporting. Analysis and commentary should be labeled and not misrepresent fact or context.
- Distinguish news from advertising and shun hybrids that blur the lines between the two.
- Recognize a special obligation to ensure that the public's business is conducted in the open and that government records are open to inspection.

Minimize Harm

Ethical journalists treat sources, subjects and colleagues as human beings deserving of respect.

Journalists should:

- Show compassion for those who may be affected adversely by news coverage. Use special sensitivity when dealing with children and inexperienced sources or subjects.

- Be sensitive when seeking or using interviews or photographs of those affected by tragedy or grief.
- Recognize that gathering and reporting information may cause harm or discomfort. Pursuit of the news is not a license for arrogance.
- Recognize that private people have a greater right to control information about themselves than do public officials and others who seek power, influence or attention. Only an overriding public need can justify intrusion into anyone's privacy.
- Show good taste. Avoid pandering to lurid curiosity.
- Be cautious about identifying juvenile suspects or victims of sex crimes.
- Be judicious about naming criminal suspects before the formal filing of charges.
- Balance a criminal suspect's fair trial rights with the public's right to be informed.

Act Independently

Journalists should be free of obligation to any interest other than the public's right to know.

Journalists should:

- Avoid conflicts of interest, real or perceived.
- Remain free of associations and activities that may compromise integrity or damage credibility.

- Refuse gifts, favors, fees, free travel and special treatment, and shun secondary employment, political involvement, public office and service in community organizations if they compromise journalistic integrity.
- Disclose unavoidable conflicts.
- Be vigilant and courageous about holding those with power accountable.
- Deny favored treatment to advertisers and special interests and resist their pressure to influence news coverage.
- Be wary of sources offering information for favors or money; avoid bidding for news.

Be Accountable

Journalists are accountable to their readers, listeners, viewers and each other.

Journalists should:

- Clarify and explain news coverage and invite dialogue with the public over journalistic conduct.
- Encourage the public to voice grievances against the news media.
- Admit mistakes and correct them promptly.
- Expose unethical practices of journalists and the news media.
- Abide by the same high standards to which they hold others.

Source: Sigma Delta Chi's first Code of Ethics was borrowed from the American Society of Newspaper Editors in 1926. In 1973, Sigma Delta Chi wrote its own code, which was revised in 1984 and 1987. The present version of the Society of Professional Journalists' Code of Ethics was adopted in September 1996.

Appendix D

Association of School Business Officials International (ASBO) Standards of Behavior

The Association of School Business Officials International (ASBO) is concerned about standards of behavior and adopted the following Standards of Ethical Conduct:

ASBO International Ethical Standards
In all activities, members shall:

1. Make the well being of students, staff, and fellow members a fundamental value in all decision-making and actions.
2. Fulfill professional responsibilities with honesty and integrity.
3. Support the principle of due process and protect the civil and human rights of all individuals.
4. Obey all local, state, and national laws.
5. Implement the policies and administrative rules and regulations of the employing organization (school district, private school and/or associated organization).

6. Pursue appropriate measures to correct those laws, policies, and regulations that are not consistent with this code of ethics.
7. Not tolerate the failure of others to act in an ethical manner and pursue appropriate measures to correct such failures.
8. Never use their positions for personal gain through political, social, religious, economic, or other influence.

ASBO International Employer Relationships

In Relationships within the School District it is expected that the School Business Administrator will:

1. Actively support the goals and objectives of the educational institution with which they work;
2. Interpret the policies and practices of their employer to the staff and to the community fairly and objectively;
3. Implement, to the best of their ability, the policies and administrative regulations of their employer;
4. Assist fellow administrators, as appropriate, in fulfilling their obligations;
5. Support a positive image of the educational institution with which they work;
6. Not publicly criticize board members, superiors, administrators, or other employees;

7. Help subordinates achieve their maximum potential through fair and just treatment;
8. Maintain confidentiality of data and information;
9. Accurately and objectively report data, in a timely fashion, to authorized agencies.[40]

---

[40] http://asbointl.org/resources/professional-standards-code-of-ethics

The Ethical Dimension of Superintendent Decision Making: A Study of AASA Members

By William C. Fensternmaker
Principal, Riverview Elementary School and Maytown Elementary School, Lancaster County, Pennsylvania

Do superintendents today more consistently select ethical choices compared with their counterparts of 25 years ago?

That was the principal question of my doctoral dissertation completed two years ago at Temple University. My research sought to update a 1968 study by long-time AASA member C. Roy Dexheimer, now superintendent of the Tompkins-Seneca-Tioga BOCES in Ithaca, N.Y. Dexheimer found superintendents frequently made choices that were inconsistent with the AASA Code of Ethics. Sadly for the state of the profession, my findings, with few exceptions, nearly duplicated those obtained a quarter century earlier.

My Format

I patterned my survey of superintendents closely after that used by Dexheimer, which he used as his dissertation at the University of Rochester. I also used the 1962 version of the

AASA Code of Ethics, though a streamlined version of the code was adopted by the association in 1981. Superintendents were asked to respond to a borderline ethical dilemma-typically a minor problem of a routine nature-designed to elicit a response or choice of action. The dilemmas approximated situations that most administrators likely would encounter at some time. Of the choices provided, only one would have been considered appropriate based on the guidelines and examples of the 1962 code.

The survey was sent to 420 randomly selected superintendents from the AASA membership rolls. Replies numbered 242, or 60.6 percent. The study collected information about the respondents' age, sex, years of experience, size of district, and salary levels.

In addition, a panel of AASA Executive Committee members completed the survey, indicating the choices that they considered "most ethical," to serve as another guide for scoring responses. The majority replies from this panel produced a second standard against which the superintendent responses were compared, resulting in two separate scores for each survey response.

Major Findings
Lack of change since 1968.

Dexheimer recorded 1,725 ethical responses on the dilemma scenarios out of a possible total of 3,630, or 47.3 percent. Using the same criteria, my study recorded 1,341 ethical replies out of a possible 2,790, or 48.1 percent. The majority of responses to both surveys were unethical, with the difference less than one percentage point from then to now, suggesting no significant change over time.

Variations relative to enrollment.

My study found, as Dexheimer did, a tendency for scores to be higher (or more ethical) for superintendents in larger school systems. Scores were as much as 10 points higher among superintendents in districts with more than 20,000 students.

Variations relative to salary.

Again affirming the Dexheimer data, my study found a strong tendency for scores to be higher among superintendents receiving the highest salaries. With the exception of a small group at the lowest salary level, scores showed a steady increase as salary increases, with the differences again as great as 10 points or more.

Variations relative to experience.

While not as pronounced as the salary and enrollment variations, my study noted a tendency for higher scores among those superintendents with fewer years of service, both in their current district and overall. Dexheimer made note of a similar tendency in his data.

Actual versus hypothetical responses.

One difference between my data and that from 1968 was noteworthy. Dexheimer found his subjects reporting the majority of their ethical replies as coming from actual experience. The recent study instead found the majority of non-ethical replies coming from actual experience. This may suggest that superintendents today are even less ethical in actual practice than they were in 1968.

Differences based upon gender.

Dexheimer could not have studied this effect since all of his subjects were male. While only 10 of the respondents in the recent study were female, the significant difference in responses between male and female superintendents is worthy of attention.

Troubling Implications

The results of the study clearly and strongly indicate that the matter of ethics in administrative decision-making still has not received adequate attention. The survey responses from superintendents nationwide showed either a severe confusion about ethical standards or a disturbing disregard of them. Probably a combination of both factors was involved in producing such disappointingly low scores.

Either superintendents are unaware of the ethical factors suffused in the issues they face or they simply do not care. Whichever is the case, the matter clearly requires attention. Dexheimer's survey data produced a nationwide ethical score of 47.3 percent. Less than half of the survey questions were answered ethically. The new survey produced a nationwide score of 48.1 percent, hardly an improvement. Even when using the AASA standard (generated from the responses of AASA Executive Committee members), which produces the most generous and optimistic result, the scores from this national sample are only 61.6 percent. In most school systems, this would earn a grade of D-minus.

These results should be cause for concern, among all parts of the education community. What is likely is that the superintendents responding to the survey failed to recognize any ethical issues in many of the situations given. What is also possible is that they follow their instincts and their experience in making decisions, and their instincts or experience may not generally take the ethical factors into consideration.

Dexheimer speculated that the larger school districts, where salary is often higher, place superintendents in positions of higher visibility and scrutiny, which would increase the societal pressure to perform ethically. The reasons for low scores, as well as the reasons for the variations among groups, are among several considerations for additional research.

But even though it would be interesting, and possibly helpful, to learn more about the explanations for these findings, there remains a concern about them at their face value. There is a need for a higher level of awareness of the ethical issues that administrators face every day, and a need for practice in both recognizing and dealing with those issues.

Suggested Actions

Given that ethical issues appear to be inadequately addressed in the day-to-day functioning of the typical school superintendent, a number of recommendations should be self-evident. My recommendations are addressed to various audiences within the education community.

To AASA.

Since the survey was conducted among members of AASA and evaluated using both an AASA code of ethics and a newer set of criteria drawn from among its officers, the association should view the findings as either a critique of the low level of attention paid to ethics by AASA or as a critique of its members' interest or awareness of the issue.

Several years ago AASA disbanded its Ethics Committee, the panel of review that would have been responsible for enforcing and interpreting the Code of Ethics. In the years that this panel was in place, few cases were brought before it, and it was very rare for the committee to find anyone in violation or impose any form of disciplinary action. This was one of the reasons for the dissolution of the committee: It seemed nearly valueless.

Consider, on the other hand, the various levels of review in place among another profession. Attorneys across the country fall under the jurisdiction of their own organization's ethics review boards, and bar associations do not shy away from the practice of disbarment. It is done perhaps infrequently, but nonetheless it is done in an effort to maintain the credibility of the profession as a whole.

Lawyers policing their own ranks, for the benefit of all, not for the protection of any individual, help to keep the profession honest (to some extent) and help to keep individual attorneys feeling accountable.

One thing that AASA should consider is reestablishing its ethics panel, but with a revitalized charge to become more aggressive, more demanding, and more believable. The profession may need to become more vocal about its position on ethical issues and more firm with its members to create a heightened sense of awareness and accountability. If members (and non-member observers) can see a strong emphasis on ethics and accountability at the national level, they will be more likely to raise their own levels of awareness and be more receptive to whatever information the association might provide.

Superintendents are extremely busy people with many priorities. In order to make them feel motivated to pay attention to this issue, they must be made to feel a personal stake in it. Currently, no source of pressure exists to make people care about it. AASA could provide the pressure.

Along with recreating the ethics panel, AASA ought to wage an aggressive information campaign. Over several years, the organization should find and use every means available to get the message to its members-that ethics is a matter of significance, that too many superintendents do not know enough about it currently, that it needs to be a factor in more administrative decisions, and that every administrator needs to receive training in the skills necessary to recognize the ethical issues common in his or her routine.

From its position as the major national organization and adviser for superintendents, AASA has a unique opportunity to provide both influence and encouragement to its constituents. It also has an obligation to meet their needs for information and assistance in their jobs. Although other groups have similar obligations and opportunities, of all the groups who can make a difference AASA stands the best chance of performing the most worthwhile service in this area.

To Training Institutions.

Prior to becoming a superintendent, most administrators undergo a lengthy period of graduate school preparation. In most of these preparation programs there are courses in law, but not always courses in ethics and how it relates to decision-making on a daily basis.

Every administrator-training program at every graduate school should implement course work in the ethical factors that relate to school and district administration, if the university has not already done so. Graduate school planners should search the available literature and obtain worthwhile materials to assemble at least one course on ethics in administration.

Such courses should be required of every prospective administrator, whether they aspire to the principalship or the central office. The ideal situation would be at least two different courses, one designed primarily for building-level administrators and another primarily for those in central office.

Although emphasis on ethics in graduate school programs is essential, it will not address the more long-term needs. Nor will it address the need that obviously exists among practicing administrators. A need also exists for ongoing in-service education on this topic.

Graduate schools need to expand their sense of mission to include those program graduates who are currently employed and trying to do their jobs after leaving the college environment. These men and women continue to be representatives of their respective institutions, and the extent to which they promote a positive image should be a matter of concern to the schools from which they have graduated. Unethical conduct from a graduate of a particular school does not reflect well on the school.

To the Education Community.

School districts, state boards, local school boards, local administrator organizations, state school board associations, county administrative units, and virtually every group that works for or with the public schools need to give serious consideration to the implications of this study. A message in these findings should call attention to an unmet need for superintendents to become more aware of themselves and their skill in recognizing ethical issues in their work roles.

To the extent that any organization is able to address this issue, all should make some effort. School boards should encourage their administrators to find and take advantage of seminars on the issue, not with any threatening tone or with suspicious intent, but for the betterment of their employees and their school district.

Local and county administrative units should seek the help of universities and national organizations with expertise in this area and secure speakers for regional seminars and training sessions. State boards should find ways to raise the awareness level, if not the anxiety level, of superintendents to encourage them to undergo training in ethics. State and national administrator associations should encourage such participation. Ethics, as an issue, does not begin to compare with such topics as inclusion, preschool education, assessment, restructuring, or site-based management, to name just a few current concerns. It will continue to have low a priority unless significant attention is given to it at every level. Then, a coordinated effort must fill the need.

This may be one of the reasons why there has been so little improvement since the earlier study. Dexheimer's research in 1968 should have prompted the kind of all-out response suggested here to raise the levels of awareness and concern and then address the need with training. But no such significant response occurred. Some articles and a few seminar speeches addressed the subject, but no concerted effort took place.

To Educational Researchers.

My study, like Dexheimer's a generation earlier, suggests a variety of interesting and worthwhile directions for additional research.

For example, it would be interesting to verify (or disprove) the implication that higher-paid superintendents apply a higher level of ethical reasoning in their decision-making process. An equally worthwhile study would examine the same phenomenon in superintendents from larger school systems. Perhaps of more value, though, would be research to determine the reasons for such differences. What is it about those who receive higher salaries or those in larger districts that cause them to respond differently?

One obvious and necessary direction for further research arises from the gender differences suggested in my work. Why do women tend to score higher on tests involving matters of morals and ethics, particularly in the field of educational administration?

The most significant research contributions would come from those studies which would further verify the degree to which superintendent decision-making is lacking in ethical foundations. My study used an existing survey. New surveys of a similar nature should be developed, presenting the same type of borderline ethical dilemmas with choices clearly identified as either ethical or non-ethical by those evaluating responses using existing codes of ethics.

More research that confirms the patterns in this study would emphasize the need for more training and education in the field of ethics.

Consideration must be given to the many factors influencing administrative decisions. Superintendents are motivated by many considerations in the choices they make, and the data reported in my research was not able to demonstrate these many forces. Additional research should determine which forces and considerations guide administrator decision-making since ethical considerations may not be a high priority.

Immediate Precautions

At the core of ethical behavior is the issue of trust. And what the profession must accept is that, as group superintendents, run the risk of becoming just another one of the many distrusted occupations. In their high-visibility roles, superintendents engender many passionate and emotional responses. They are often hated or feared. But their continued success in a school district depends, to some extent, on their credibility. They must be believed, or they become ineffectual.

As the American people become increasingly skeptical of all persons in positions of power and authority, it will become more and more necessary for superintendents to know and conscientiously apply ethical principles in their work roles. The alternative will be a gradual degradation of the profession as a whole-a loss of trust eventually extending not only to superintendents, but to the entire public school system that they represent.

Before public attitudes begin this potential slide, we should do whatever we can to prevent it and to assist each other to become more sensitive to the issues that would cause it.

Source:
The School Administrator
American Association of School Administrators (AASA)
October 1996, Number 8, Volume 53.

(Reprinted with permission from *School Administrator* magazine, a publication of AASA, the School Superintendents Association.)

About the Author

Clarence G. Oliver, Jr., Ed.D.
Emeritus Professor and Former Dean of Education
Oral Roberts University, Tulsa, Oklahoma
and
Retired Superintendent of Schools
Broken Arrow (Oklahoma) Public Schools

Clarence G. Oliver, Jr., has enjoyed work in several career fields. He has been a teacher, journalist, Army officer, school administrator, newspaper editor and publisher, author, university professor and dean of a university college of education.

Most recently the Dean of Education at Oral Roberts University and named by the university regents as an Emeritus Professor in 1999, he is best known for his work as superintendent of one of Oklahoma's fastest-growing school districts, Broken Arrow, where he was a school administrator for 30 years.

Prior to becoming a school administrator in Broken Arrow, he was managing editor of the *Broken Arrow Ledger* and other newspapers owned by McWilliams Publications, Inc., and after retiring from the superintendent's position in July, 1992, he joined Retherford Publications, Inc., as publisher of the *Broken Arrow Scout* and assistant to owner and publisher Bill Retherford, publisher of several other Tulsa area newspapers. During his years as Dean at Oral Roberts University, he continued as an editorial writer and contributing editor for the *Broken Arrow Daily Ledger*.

He continues with the University work, serving as an Emeritus Professor, and a guest adjunct Professor in the ORU Graduate School of Education (Educational Leadership Studies Program).

An officer and member of several state, regional and national organizations, active in church, community and civic work, he is a former member of the Oklahoma State Board of Vocational-Technical Education, serving during the administrations of three Governors.

A veteran of the Korean War, Oliver was a Master Sergeant in a front-line Infantry Company during the 1951-1952 Second Korean Winter Campaign. After receiving a direct commission as a Second Lieutenant, he continued with military service in active and reserve command and staff capacities for 30 years and is a retired U.S. Army Infantry Major with a specialty in military intelligence as a psychological operations officer.

He attended East Central University, Oklahoma State University, the University of Oklahoma, the University of Tulsa, and the United States Army Infantry School, Ft. Benning, Ga. He received his master and doctor's degrees from the University of Tulsa, where he received the Distinguished Alumni recognition in 1986.

He was inducted in the Oklahoma Educators Hall of Fame in 1989; was honored as the Distinguished Alumnus of East Central University in 1991; and, in June 1999, he was recognized by the Oklahoma Association of School Administrators for more than four decades of service to education with the presentation of the *"Lifetime Achievement Award for Distinguished Service to Education."*

Active in church and civic work in his community, he is a member of Boards of Directors of several civic, business and professional organizations, including serving on Boards of Directors of Cancer Treatment Centers of America at Southwestern Regional Medical Center, Tulsa; Junior Achievement of Oklahoma, Inc., the Broken Arrow Community Foundation, Thunderbird Youth Academy Foundation, Broken Arrow Historical Society Foundation, and Keep Broken Arrow Beautiful, Inc.

He and his late wife, Vinita, are parents of three children, grandparents to seven grandchildren and five great-grandchildren.

Acknowledgments—

There are so many people who have provided encouragement and assistance to me during the days of research and writing of this book that I most certainly will overlook someone and fail to give proper acknowledgment to all who deserve my words of appreciation.

For any such unintentional oversight, I sincerely apologize.

I am very grateful to three very dedicated school executives who form the Ethics Committee of OASA— Chairman Rick Garrison, Superintendent of Schools, Cheyenne Public Schools; Dr. Jim Beckham, Superintendent of Schools, Blanchard Public Schools; and Cliff Johnson, Superintendent of Schools, Latta Public Schools. They graciously gathered for several meetings to offer wise suggestions and encouragement to proceed with this project. Their input was invaluable.

Had it not been for the insistence of Steven Crawford, Executive Director, OASA and CCOSA; former superintendent of schools of Byng and Rolf Public Schools, and the encouragement of members of the Boards of Directors of the administrator organizations, this work would not have been started. Their encouragement is appreciated. I am hopeful they are not disappointed in the finished product.

Three very talented school leaders with extensive school finance experience helped me "tip-toe" through the complicated areas of proper management of school resources. For the advice and counsel of Dr. Pam Deering, Executive Director, Oklahoma Association of School Administrators and past-Superintendent of Schools, Mid-Del School District; Dr. Patricia (Trish) Williams, Chief Financial Officer, Tulsa Public Schools, and Debbie Jacoby, Chief Financial Officer, Union Public Schools, I am deeply indebted.

Dr. Kenneth Hancock, Professor and Assistant Dean, College of Education, Northeastern State University, has extensively researched Oklahoma's Constitution, statutes and regulations concerning school law and school finance, and is recognized as an authority in both fields. School administrators who studied with him and have been mentored by him are fortunate indeed. During the months of writing, rewriting and editing of this book, I have been privileged to listen to his counsel. I am grateful for his assistance . . . and friendship.

Retired Oklahoma State Senator and Brigadier General Gerald Wright, a former Air Force jet fighter pilot, retired commander of the Oklahoma Air National Guard, and long-time friend, provided encouragement and persistently urged me to "finish this book" for school administrators. He offered reflections on the "intent" of some sections of Oklahoma Law. His brotherly advice has been invaluable.

Dr. Kerry Roberts, Associate Professor, Stephen F. Austin State University, Nachadoges, Texas; a former valued member of my administrative team at Broken Arrow Public Schools, and later a faculty with whom I was privileged to serve at Oral Roberts University, has been a constant encourager through the years. His long-distance support has been very helpful as I contemplated how to express some thoughts expressed in this book. He is an accomplished author of several books and articles in educational journals; and, I am appreciative of his permitting me to "lift" a portion from one of his books for inclusion in a chapter of this book.

I would be remiss if I did not give credit to Dr. Jim Myers, Graduate Professor of Educational Administration, Oral Roberts University, and a former long-time Tecumseh, Oklahoma, superintendent of schools, for helping me "remain current" on critical educational issues. I appreciate his regularly inviting me to join in discussion with the students from across the nation and other nations who are in Dr. Myer's graduate education classes. Those guest speaking opportunities, with the in-depth questioning by talented school administrators who are about to complete their doctoral degrees, have forced me to carefully think about my positions and opinions on issues related to the role of school leaders.

For all the others who have inquired about "when?" and expressed so many encouraging words through the many months when this has been "a work in progress," I also express my appreciation.

All of you are wonderful, gracious friends. I struggle with how to express appreciation for all the support. The two small words, "Thank You," seem so inadequate; but, until I can find better words, these are written to each of you with my sincere gratitude.

Clarence G. Oliver, Jr.
Broken Arrow,
Oklahoma
2015

Need for Ethics in School Districts

"Few U.S. school districts employ an ethics officer, and it's unclear how many have formal ethics codes. . . . It's not that wrongdoing is on the upswing. But in this era of budget cutting and high-stakes accountability, when critics may raise suspicion about what's really happening with the money, a school district that leads with clarity about ethics can bolster community trust. As a bonus, it also can strengthen employee morale and motivation."

—Joan McRobbie
senior research associate, WestEd, San Francisco, California
author, Contagious Effects of a District's Ethics Code
School Administrator, AASA

Inexperienced Leaders

"Dr. Oliver . . . traces the problem of unethical behavior among some school leaders, in part, to the lack of experience he sees in those being hired today by school boards to fill superintendencies. Educators who entered the field (a few decades ago) and rose through the ranks to become superintendents are retiring in waves. The vacancies they create are not drawing the quantity and quality of experienced administrators eager to assume the top berth (and) may not have the training, experience or strength to stand up to the pressures being forced on them. Dr. Oliver contends that those entering without much experience in key decision-making roles are 'more likely to fall into the trap of what appears to be an innocent proposal without considering the underlying ethical issues, more inclined to go with the first decision that comes to mind . . . [and] less likely to look at the consequences of unethical behavior.'"

—Priscilla Pardini, Shorewood, Wisconsin
author, Ethics in the Superintendency
School Administrator, AASA

Bibliography & References

Books

Brown, H. Jackson. *Life's Little Instruction Book.* Nashville. Rutledge Hill Press, 1991.

Business Ethics: Readings and Cases in Corporate Morality. New York: McGraw-Hill, 1995.

Day, Louis A. *Ethics in Media Communications: Cases and Controversies.* Belmont, CA: Wadsworth Publishing Co., 1999.

Dienhart, John William. *Institutions, Business, and Ethics: A Text with Cases and Readings.* New York: Oxford University Press, 1999.

Essex, Nathan L. *A Teacher's Pocket Guide to School Law.* Boston: Pearson, 2010.

Hauan, Martin. *How to Win Elections Without Hardly Cheatin' At All,* Midwest Political Publications, Oklahoma City, Oklahoma, 1983.

Kallman, Ernest A. *Ethical Decision Making and Information Technology.* New York: McGraw-Hill, 1996.

Kultgen, John. *Ethics and Professionalism,* University of Pennsylvania Press: Philadelphia, 1988.

Maxwell, William, *If I Were Twenty-One: Tips From a Business Veteran.* Philadelphia and London: J, B. Lippincott, 1917.

Media Ethics: Issues and Cases. Boston, MA: McGraw-Hill, 1998.

Owens, James. *Business Ethics.* Arlington, VA: Executive Publications Inc., 1989.

School Laws of Oklahoma, Oklahoma State Department of Education. Oklahoma City, 2014.

Pfeiffer, Raymond S. *Ethics on the Job: Cases and Strategies*. Belmont, CA: Wadsworth Publishing Co., 1999.

Roberts, Kerry; Sampson, Pauline, and Glenn, Jeremy. *Daily Devotionals for Superintendents*, Nacogdoches, Texas: Stephen F. Austin State University Press, 2014.

Stoppard, Tom. *Rosencrantz and Guildenstern are Dead (Play)*. New York. Grove/Atlantic, Inc., 1976.

U.S. Office of Government Ethics. *Do it Right: An Ethics Handbook for Executive Branch Employees*. Washington, DC: U.S. Government Printing Office, 1995.

U.S. Office of Government Ethicsm. *Standards of Ethical Conduct for Employees of the Executive Branch*. Washington, DC: U.S. Government Printing Office, 1999.

WASBO Handbook. Madison: Wisconsin Association of School Business Officials, 2000.

Wood, Craig R. *Principles of School Business Management*. Reston, Virginia: Association of School Business Officials International, 1986.

Fensternmaker, William C. *The Ethical Dimension of Superintendent Decision Making: A Study of AASA Members*. The School Administrator, American Association of School Administrators (AASA), October 1996, Number 8, Volume 53, 1996.

Markkula Center for Applied Ethics. *Approaching Ethics*. Ethics Connection. Santa Clara, California. Santa Clara University. World Wide Web: http://scuish.scu.edu/Ethics, 1999.

Mooney, Richard L. *Ethics Forum: Cases and Comments*. Hauppage, NY: National Association of Educational Buyers, 1996.

The Holy Bible, New International Version, Grand Rapids: Zondervan House, 1984.

Taylor, Herbert. "About Us," The 4-Way Test Association, Inc., Retrieved July 2, 2011. Rotary International. Evanston, IL., 2011

Velasquez, Manuel G. *Business Ethics: Concepts and Cases*. London: Prentice Hall International, 1998.

Velasquez, Manuel G. ; Andre, Claire; Shanks, Thomas, and Meyer, Michael J. *Approaching Ethics.* Markkula Center of Applied Ethics, Santa Clara, 2014.

Wood, Craig R. *Principles of School Business Management,* ASBO International, 1986.

Wisconsin Association of School Business Officials. Handbook, 2000.

Other

Corporate Watch. *Commercialism in the Classroom: The Education Industry: The Corporate Takeover of Public Schools 1-2,* http://www.corpwatch.org/trac/feature/education/commercial, 1999.

Corporate Watch. *Captive Kids: A Report on Commercial Pressures on Kids at School. The Corporate Takeover of Public Schools 1-2,* http://www.corpwatch.org/trac/feature/education/commercial, 1999.

Crowder, Mark A. and Brown, D. Diane. *Ethical Integrity and the Supply Chain.* NAPM Newsletter, National Association of Purchasing Management. http://www.napm-dv.org/newsletter/articles/feb., 1999.

Education Week. *Schools Look Beyond Budgets for Outside Income*: 1-3, December 7, 1994.

Ladd, John. *Introduction. Codes of Ethics Online,* Center for the Study of Ethics in Professions (CSEP): http://csep.iit.edu/codes/coe, 1999.

Little, Miles & Fearnside, Michael. *On Trust.* <u>On Line Journal of Ethics</u>. Houston. Center for Business Ethics Studies, University of St. Thomas. www.stthom.edu/cbes., 1997

Luegenbiehl, Heinz. *Introduction.* Center for the Study of Ethics in Professions (CSEP). Chicago.Institute of Technology. http://csep.iit.edu/codes/coe/Introduction.html, 1999.

NIGP: The Institute for Public Procuremen. Herndon, VA, http://www.naepnet.org/CodeOfEthics

Obama, President Barrack, U.S. Office of the President. *Prescribing Standards of Ethical Conduct for Government Officers and Employees.* Executive Order 13490, Washington, DC, January 21, 2009.

Pastore, Michael. *Businesses Moving Toward Electronic Purchasing.* CyberAtlas, INT Media Group, Incorporated. http://cyberatlas. internet.com/markets, 1999.

Pardini, Priscilla, Ethics *in the Superintendency,* The School Administrator, American Association of School Administrators, Arlington, VA, September 2004.

McRobbie, Joan, *Contagious Effects of a District's Ethics Code,* The School Administrator, American Association of School Administrators, Arlington, VA, November 2010.

UW-Milwaukee Center for the Analysis of Commercialism In Education. *Commercialism in Americas Schools Continues Upward Trend* 1-3.

http://www.uwm.edu/Dept./CACE/kidsreport/cashingpressrelease. html, 1999.

CPSIA information can be obtained
at www.ICGtesting.com
Printed in the USA
LVHW032248090723
751960LV00001B/45

9 781504 962070